Preparing for the State Exam

Situational Problems for Cosmetology

Linnea Lindquist
Minneapolis Technical College

Milady Publishing Company
(A Division of Delmar Publishers, Inc.)
3 Columbia Circle
Albany, New York 12212

NOTICE TO THE READER

Publisher does not warrant or guarantee any of the products described herein or perform any independent analysis in connection with any of the product information contained herein. Publisher does not assume, and expressly disclaims, any obligation to obtain and include information other than that provided to it by the manufacturer.

The reader is expressly warned to consider and adopt all safety precautions that might be indicated by the activities herein and to avoid all potential hazards. By following the instructions contained herein, the reader willingly assumes all risks in connection with such instructions.

The Publisher makes no representation or warranties of any kind, including but not limited to, the warranties of fitness for particular purpose or merchantability, nor are any such representations implied with respect to the material set forth herein, and the publisher takes no responsibility with respect to such material. The publisher shall not be liable for any special, consequential, or exemplary damages resulting, in whole or part, from the readers' use of, or reliance upon, this material.

Printed in the United States of America
12 13 14 15 116 XXX 05 04 03 02 01 00 99

For more information, contact Milady, 3 Columbia Circle, PO Box 15015, Albany, NY 12212-0515; or find us on the World Wide Web at http://www.Milady.com

Library of Congress Cataloging-in-Publication Data:

ISBN: 156253-019-4

Contents

Preparing for the State Exam

Preface

Preparing for the State Exam: Situational Problems for Cosmetology is a new and innovative book of test questions for cosmetology students. The test questions are situational or practical items that require analytical thinking by students. When taking such a test, students must be able to apply their theoretical and practical knowledge to the situation and/or problem posed in the test question. This book provides an opportunity for students to deal with the kind of real-life problems and decisions that they will confront every day in their careers as cosmetology professionals.

As many states are increasing the number of situational items on their tests, it is important that students be familiar with this type of test question. This book provides instructors and students with situational tests for practice. *Preparing for the State Exam: Situational Problems for Cosmetology* is designed to complement other review/exam books, as a convenient source of test questions for classroom use, or for use on its own.

Students are to answer each item in this exam book. Items can be corrected and/or rated during class or individual discussions, or on an independent study basis. Answers to the tests and ratings of student scores are included in this book.

SPECIFIC INFORMATION ABOUT THIS BOOK

1. This book was designed to reflect the theoretical and practical information found in *Milady's STANDARD Textbook of Cosmetology*.

2. Some of the information on items in this exam book may not be found in *Milady's STANDARD Textbook of Cosmetology*.

3. All situations in this book are hypothetical.

4. Proper names used in the situations reflect a multi-cultural and gender-fair balance.

5. Some test items require that the students analyze the information that they already know, and then apply that knowledge to the test item in front of them. For example, there are test questions in this book that contain a list (choices 1, 2, 3, 4, 5) from which two or more are correct. These are then reflected in the choices (A, B, C, D). This type of test item provides an involved challenge for cosmetology students!

6. Some "situations" are used for more than one test question. For example, students may be asked to read one situation, and then answer the three or four following test questions based on that one situation.

7. The contents of this new test book follow, chapter by chapter, the contents of *Milady's STANDARD Textbook of Cosmetology*.

TEST/EXAM WRITING HINTS FOR INSTRUCTORS (MULTIPLE-CHOICE)

When writing and designing tests for students, it is important that the end result be a fair, easily understood, and clean test. If you write your own tests for your students, here are some suggestions that may help:

1. If a stem sentence ends in a colon, the choices should have a period after each of them (because they are ending a sentence), such as :

   A. choice a .
   B. choice b .
   C. choice c .
   D. choice d .

2. If a stem sentence ends in a question mark, the choices do not have a period after them, such as ?

   A. choice a
   B. choice b
   C. choice c
   D. choice d

3. The letters **A, B, C, D** denoting choices should all be in capital letters (not in small letters, such as a, b, c, d).

4. If the stem sentence ends in a reversal/negative, that specific word should be capitalized and in bold print, such as the word **EXCEPT**.

5. The entire test item and all of its choices should be included on the same page. A test item should never start on one page and end on the next page. All of the information the student needs should be together.

6. If the choices include numbers, the numbers should be written in either ascending or descending order. They should not be mixed up. Examples:

Okay:	*Okay:*	*Not okay:*
A. 1	A. 4	A. 3
B. 2	B. 3	B. 1
C. 3	C. 2	C. 4
D. 4	D. 1	D. 2

7. Choices (A, B, C, D) should NOT have repeating words in them. If all of the choices have the same word, that word should be included in the stem sentence, and not repeated for every choice.

Correct example:

In order to interact with other salon staff members, a cosmetologist must have effective _______________ skills.

A. foreign language
B. client listening
C. communication
D. ordering

Incorrect example:

In order to interact with other salon staff members, a cosmetologist must have effective:

A. foreign language skills .
B. client listening skills .
C. communication skills .
D. ordering skills .

Any test that is presented to students should be accurate, fair, and easy to understand. Testing through examination is a measurement or evaluation of student's learning. Hopefully, the above hints will make test designing and writing easier for you, the instructor!

Linnea M. Lindquist
Minneapolis Technical College

Acknowledgments

Thanks to the following who helped edit and review the material in this book:

Mary Holley
Fridley, MN

Vivian Martinez
San Jose City College
San Jose, CA

Eileen Morrissey
Maison de Paris Beauty College
Cherry Hill, NJ

James Overstreet
International Beauty College
Garland, TX

Jacob Yahm
Lauderdale Lakes, FL

Introduction

1. Dominique applies facial cosmetics to enhance her client's appearance. Specifically, Dominique is a/an:
   A. cosmetic chemist.
   B. salon owner.
   C. makeup artist.
   D. educational specialist. ____

2. Porat, who works with Dominique, offers treatments for the health of the skin. Porat is a:
   A. makeup artist.
   B. skin care specialist.
   C. competition champion.
   D. retail salesperson. ____

3. A cosmetologist who specializes in choosing, mixing, and applying various dyes to her/his client's hair is called a/an:
   A. salon owner.
   B. hair colorist.
   C. esthetician.
   D. nail technician. ____

4. Imagine that you are at a national cosmetology trade show. Brita is on stage demonstrating new hair techniques. Brita is a:
   A. stage person.
   B. chemical technician.
   C. trade show expert.
   D. platform artist. ____

5. Celia works for a large manufacturing company performing research and evaluating new products. Celia is a/an:
   A. cosmetic chemist.
   B. sales representative.
   C. publisher.
   D. esthetician. ____

6. Dennis enters many haircutting contests each year. He has won nine awards so far in his career as a:

   A. nail technician.
   B. haircutting demonstrator.
   C. competition champion.
   D. salon owner. ___

7. Keith is a cosmetology instructor. Another name for this career is:

   A. educator.
   B. field technician.
   C. demonstrator.
   D. author. ___

8. Emma is a licensed cosmetologist. The field of cosmetology includes which of the following areas of study?

   1. hair
   2. skin
   3. nails

   A. 1 only
   B. 1 and 3
   C. 2 and 3
   D. 1, 2, and 3 ___

9. Curtis is licensed in his state to perform services on the nails. He is a/an:

   A. manicurist.
   B. esthetician.
   C. cosmetologist.
   D. electrologist. ___

10. Helen is licensed in her state to (only) perform services on the skin. She is licensed as a/an:

    A. manicurist.
    B. esthetician.
    C. cosmetologist.
    D. electrologist. ___

1. Your Professional Image

1. Charles exercises daily. His exercise does all of the following **EXCEPT**:

   A. strengthens his muscles.
   B. decreases his heart's functioning.
   C. improves his circulation.
   D. increases his flexibility. ____

2. The client who has just arrived smells offensive—this person obviously has not taken a bath or shower lately. This situation refers to your client's:

   A. public hygiene.
   B. personal grooming.
   C. personal hygiene.
   D. public sanitation. ____

3. If a cosmetologist's feet are sore, he or she will have a difficult time standing up throughout the day. To avoid this problem, you should wear shoes that have __________ heels.

   A. high
   B. low
   C. 5 inch
   D. 6 inch ____

4. Your pedicure client's name is Mavis. Corns and ingrown nails have recently appeared on her feet. These are to be treated by:

   A. a podiatrist.
   B. Mavis.
   C. the salon manager.
   D. a nail technician. ____

5. Which of the following are included in a cosmetologist's physical presentation?

   1. posture
   2. foot condition
   3. walk
   4. movements

   A. 1 and 2
   B. 2 and 3
   C. 1, 3, and 4
   D. 1, 2, 3, and 4 ____

6. Erin, a cosmetologist and co-worker of yours, has poor posture. You think she should improve her posture, and you plan to discuss this with her. One of the advantages of good posture that you should point out to Erin is that it:

   A. decreases circulation.
   B. increases activity of the sweat glands.
   C. decreases the image of confidence.
   D. helps to prevent fatigue. ____

7. Bradley is cutting his client's hair. While he is doing this, his body weight should be distributed:

   A. evenly over both of his feet.
   B. toward the client, or toward Bradley's back.
   C. away from the client, or toward Bradley's front.
   D. toward his toes. ____

8. When Marilyn is practicing good posture, her abdomen should be:

   A. rounded.
   B. protruding.
   C. bent over.
   D. flat. ____

9. When performing a manicure, the nail technician should keep his or her knees:

   A. on the side of the manicure table.
   B. 6 inches apart.
   C. close together.
   D. straight, not bent. ____

SITUATION FOR ITEMS 10–12:

Everyone in the salon agrees that Laurel has a great personality.

10. Which of the following are part of an individual's personality?

    1. attitude
    2. public hygiene
    3. thoughts
    4. inner feelings
    5. sanitation techniques
    6. values

    A. 1, 2, 3, and 4
    B. 1, 3, 4, and 6
    C. 1, 3, 5, and 6
    D. 2, 4, 5, and 6 ____

11. Laurel has shown, or expressed, her personality in many ways. All of the following are ways to express one's personality **EXCEPT**:

    A. school grades.
    B. facial expressions.
    C. voice.
    D. action. ____

12. One aspect of Laurel's personality is that she is always thoughtful of others. This is referred to as:

    A. a sense of humor.
    B. emotional control.
    C. mannerisms.
    D. good manners. ____

---

13. Avery constantly twirls the hair that hangs down on his forehead. This twirling is considered to be one of Avery's:

    A. emotional controls.
    B. disorders.
    C. facial expressions.
    D. mannerisms. ____

14. Treating your client Martha fairly, responsibly, and honestly are characteristics of good:

    A. hygiene.
    B. ethics.
    C. sanitation techniques.
    D. nonverbal communication. ____

15. In order to interact with other salon staff members, a cosmetologist must have effective __________ skills.

    A. foreign language
    B. client listening
    C. communication
    D. ordering ___

16. Ken is studying human relations. This area of study includes:

    A. the psychology of getting along well with others.
    B. the physiology of the body.
    C. the psychology of understanding yourself.
    D. the anatomy of the body. ___

SITUATION FOR ITEMS 17–18:

Your client Ms. Allen has just entered the salon. Her tone of voice and body language tell you that she is not very happy.

17. You are to greet her:

    A. by name.
    B. without using her name.
    C. in 20 minutes, after she has calmed down.
    D. angrily. ___

18. You should:

    A. ignore her bad mood because it will go away.
    B. tell her she is crabby today.
    C. pay attention to her bad mood and try to change it.
    D. refuse to perform the service. ___

---

19. Carl is early to the salon each morning. Before the clients arrive, he checks the supplies and prepares for the clients he'll have that day. This is called:

    A. unorganized.
    B. time management.
    C. personal hygiene.
    D. inefficiency. ___

20. Rich is considered to be a very professional cosmetologist because he chooses his topics of conversations with his clients carefully. Rich would be considered very unprofessional if he spoke to his clients about:

   1. other clients
   2. the poor workmanship of other cosmetologists
   3. yesterday's ball game
   4. his personal problems
   5. the weather forecast for the weekend

   A. 1, 3, and 4
   B. 1, 4, and 5
   C. 1, 2, and 5
   D. 1, 2, and 4

___

2. Bacteriology

SITUATION FOR ITEMS 1–7:

Melissa works as a cosmetologist at Countryside Hair Salon. She has had a sore throat for the past two days. Her doctor confirmed that she has strep throat. Carol owns and manages the salon. A week later, Carol's son Daniel gets strep throat, too, even though he has not seen Melissa for months.

1. Why should Melissa stay home from work?

   A. to finish her housework
   B. for her personal mental health
   C. to protect the public's health
   D. to watch Carol's son Daniel ____

2. Melissa's strep throat is considered to be:

   A. a natural immunity.
   B. contagious.
   C. an acquired immunity.
   D. not contagious. ____

3. What causes this type of sore throat?

   A. a virus
   B. pathogenic bacteria
   C. non-pathogenic bacteria
   D. penicillin ____

4. Carol did not get sick. Why? Because:

   A. of her natural immune system.
   B. she has no white blood cells.
   C. her sweat glands function improperly.
   D. her body has no immune system. ____

5. Why did Daniel get sick? Because:

   A. he has never had strep throat.
   B. he is considered to be a parasite.
   C. he has no breaks in his skin.
   D. he was more susceptible. ___

6. In this situation, who is the carrier of this infection?

   A. Melissa
   B. Carol
   C. Daniel
   D. no one ___

7. How could Melissa have gotten strep throat? Through:
   1. her mouth.
   2. her sanitized comb.
   3. a break in her skin.
   4. her clothing.
   5. a common drinking cup.

   A. 1, 3, and 5
   B. 1, 3, and 4
   C. 1, 2, and 4
   D. 2, 3, and 5 ___

SITUATION FOR ITEMS 8–9:

Melvin is having a consultation with his client Valerie. While talking with her, he notices that she has pediculosis.

8. What should Melvin do?

   A. continue with the scheduled service
   B. soak her nails in a disinfectant
   C. shampoo her hair
   D. not perform the scheduled service ___

9. What is the common name for pediculosis?

   A. itch mite
   B. brittle nails
   C. head lice
   D. ringworm ___

SITUATION FOR ITEMS 10–14:

Wendy, Patrick, and Lance are brothers and sister. Wendy has blood poisoning; Patrick has itch mites; and Lance has facial pimples.

10. What type of infection does Wendy have?

    A. parasitic
    B. local
    C. general
    D. viral ___

11. What type of bacteria causes Wendy's blood poisoning?

    A. streptococci
    B. diplococci
    C. staphylococci
    D. spirilla ___

12. What type of infection does Patrick have?

    A. plant parasitic
    B. animal parasitic
    C. viral
    D. mitosis ___

13. Patrick's infection is considered to be:

    A. communicable.
    B. bacilli.
    C. flagella-driven.
    D. noncontagious. ___

14. Lance's pimples are considered to be ______________ infections.

    A. spore-forming
    B. general
    C. viral
    D. local ___

SITUATION FOR ITEMS 15–17:

Leroy's uncle had typhoid fever during World War II.

15. What type of bacteria causes typhoid fever?

    A. spirilla
    B. staphylococci
    C. bacilla
    D. streptococci ___

16. What is the shape of this type of bacteria?

 A. round
 B. spiral
 C. triangular
 D. rod

___

17. This type of bacteria has flagella on it. Flagella help bacteria to:

 A. move.
 B. divide.
 C. separate.
 D. multiply.

___

---

18. The two phases in the life cycle of bacteria are:

 1. spore-forming stage
 2. parasitic stage
 3. spirilla-forming stage
 4. vegetative stage

 A. 1 and 3
 B. 1 and 4
 C. 2 and 3
 D. 3 and 4

___

19. Jackie's friend has syphilis. What type of bacteria causes syphilis?

 A. cocci
 B. bacilli
 C. spirilla
 D. diplococci

___

20. Evelyn's doctor has prescribed penicillin for her illness. The doctor informs her that this drug comes from bacteria. What type of bacteria would this be?

 A. harmful
 B. disease-producing
 C. pathogenic
 D. non-pathogenic

___

3. Sterilization and Sanitation

1. Gary's combs and brushes are dirty. What procedure should he follow to sanitize them?
   1. remove hair from them
   2. immerse them in a disinfectant solution
   3. store them in a closed container
   4. wash them in hot, soapy water
   5. rinse them thoroughly

   A. 1, 4, 2, 3, 5
   B. 1, 4, 5, 2, 3
   C. 3, 5, 1, 4, 2
   D. 4, 1, 5, 3, 2 ____

2. To sanitize her soiled metal scissors, Gina uses:

   A. an antiseptic.
   B. alum.
   C. alcohol.
   D. ultra violet rays. ____

3. At Betsy's Beauty Salon, sanitation is done by ____________ methods.

   A. antiseptic
   B. physical
   C. chemical
   D. steam ____

4. While frosting her client's hair, Lynn drops her only metal crochet hook on the floor. She has not finished pulling strands of hair through the cap. What should she do before continuing to use it?

   A. sanitize it with 70% alcohol
   B. wipe it off with a clean towel
   C. wash it with hot, soapy water
   D. sanitize it with 3% hydrogen peroxide ____

5. Nicole, owner of the salon, is buying disinfectant for her salon. Which of the following disinfectant qualities should she consider when making her purchase? That it be:
   1. irritating to the skin.
   2. convenient to prepare.
   3. noncorrosive.
   4. nonirritating to the skin.
   5. antiseptic strength.

   A. 1, 2, and 4
   B. 2, 3, and 4
   C. 2, 3, and 5
   D. 3, 4, and 5 ____

6. Frank is placing his brushes in a wet sanitizer. What else is in the wet sanitizer?

   A. an antiseptic
   B. ultra violet rays
   C. a fumigant tablet
   D. a disinfectant solution ____

7. What size should Frank's wet sanitizer be?

   A. large enough to immerse his implements
   B. large enough to hold 1 quart of solution
   C. 12 inches high
   D. large enough to hold 1 gallon of solution ____

SITUATION FOR ITEMS 8–11:

Felicia stores her clean perm rods in a dry sanitizer. Emily stores her clean combs in an ultra violet ray sanitizer.

8. Which of the following is an example of a dry sanitizer?

   A. a container with a disinfectant solution
   B. an open-weave basket with a cover
   C. a glass sterilizer jar containing an antiseptic
   D. an airtight cabinet ____

9. Felicia's dry sanitizer contains:

   A. alum powder.
   B. a fumigant.
   C. sodium hypochlorite.
   D. quats. ____

10. Emily's sanitizer contains:

    A. infrared rays.
    B. ultra violet rays.
    C. alcohol.
    D. a disinfectant solution. ___

11. Emily may keep her clean combs in her sanitizer:

    A. until she uses them.
    B. for a maximum of 10 minutes.
    C. for a maximum of 20 minutes.
    D. with her soiled combs. ___

SITUATION FOR ITEMS 12–15:

Brad uses sodium hypochlorite as his sanitizing agent/chemical.

12. The common name for sodium hypochlorite is:

    A. iodine.
    B. ammonia.
    C. bleach.
    D. antiseptic. ___

13. Brad uses a 10% solution of chlorine to sanitize his implements. For how many minutes must his implements be immersed in this solution in order to destroy bacteria?

    A. 5
    B. 10
    C. 15
    D. 20 ___

14. One of the advantages for Brad in choosing this chemical is that it:

    A. is in tablet form.
    B. can be used on the skin.
    C. is good for metal implements.
    D. destroys viruses. ___

15. When mixing this chemical, Brad should follow the directions/instructions given by:

    A. the manufacturer.
    B. his boss.
    C. the state examiner.
    D. his instructor. ___

SITUATION FOR ITEMS 16–17:

Beverly is the manager of a cosmetology salon. Among her sanitation supplies are two containers of alcohol. One is 70% ethyl alcohol and the other contains 99% isopropyl alcohol.

16. Alcohol is used in Beverly's salon to sanitize which of the following implements/tools?

 1. combs
 2. brushes
 3. scissors/shears
 4. perm rods
 5. metal cuticle nippers
 6. electrodes

 A. 1, 2, and 5
 B. 2, 3, and 6
 C. 3, 5, and 6
 D. 3, 4, and 5 ___

17. The strength of 99% isopropyl alcohol compared with 70% ethyl alcohol is:

 A. the same.
 B. 10% less.
 C. greater.
 D. 29% less. ___

---

18. Clark is cleaning the salon's bathrooms, sinks, and floors. The product he is using has a disinfectant ingredient in it. This specific ingredient is:

 A. hydrogen peroxide.
 B. aniline.
 C. hydroxide.
 D. creosol. ___

19. The salon's nail technician has completed one manicure and her next manicure client is waiting. What is the nail technician to do to her only finger bowl before starting her second manicure?

 A. use an antiseptic spray on it
 B. rinse it
 C. sanitize it
 D. wipe it out with paper towels ___

20. A salon's sanitizing chemicals should be stored safely and:

    A. be accessible to clients.
    B. in a hot place.
    C. with their caps/tops off.
    D. labeled correctly. ___

21. The measures used in Andre's Salon to protect public health and to prevent the spread of diseases are ____________ measures.

    A. personal grooming
    B. physical presentation
    C. personal hygiene
    D. public sanitation ___

SITUATION FOR ITEMS 22–24:

The sanitizing agent/chemical that Liz uses in her salon is quaternary ammonium compounds.

22. Liz mixes one part of quats to 1,000 parts of water. Using this strength, her minimum immersion time should be in the range of ________ minutes.

    A. 0–2
    B. 1–5
    C. 20–30
    D. 40–60 ___

23. Liz likes these compounds because they are:
    1. fast
    2. odorless
    3. unstable
    4. expensive
    5. stable

    A. 1, 2, and 5
    B. 1, 2, and 3
    C. 2, 4, and 5
    D. 3, 4, and 5 ___

24. When Liz buys this chemical, she asks for it by its nickname, which is:

    A. ammonia.
    B. alum.
    C. quats.
    D. Q.A.C. ___

---

25. Bill's favorite sanitizing agent is formalin. He likes it because he can use it as either an antiseptic or a disinfectant. A 10%–25% solution is disinfectant strength. To mix it at an antiseptic strength to use on the skin, Bill will mix it into a solution of:

    A. 40%.
    B. 30%.
    C. 11%.
    D. 5%. ___

4. Properties of the Scalp and Hair

SITUATION FOR ITEMS 1–2:

Your client Ms. Hoa Lan is at the salon for a tint retouch. During the consultation, Ms. Lan states that she needs her "roots" colored.

1. Ms. Lan's reference to "roots" is incorrect because the hair root is:

   A. the first inch of hair extending from the scalp.
   B. the hair extending beyond the first inch.
   C. located beneath the skin's surface.
   D. the first one to three inches of hair. ___

2. Which of the following correctly refers to the hair that Ms. Lan needs tinted?

   A. cold shaft
   B. new growth
   C. hair root
   D. papilla ___

SITUATION FOR ITEMS 3–6:

While cutting Reggie's hair, you notice that his hair grows out from his scalp in certain directions. The hair at his neck grows upward; the hair at his crown grows in a circular direction; and at his front hairline, he has a tuft of hair that stands up.

3. The natural flow, or direction, of Reggie's hair all over his head is his hair:

   A. stream.
   B. density.
   C. whorl.
   D. diameter. ___

4. The pocketlike depression in the skin from which Reggie's hair grows is the hair:

   A. medulla.
   B. follicle.
   C. shaft.
   D. papilla. ___

5. The tuft of hair at Reggie's front hairline is called a:

   A. whorl.
   B. hair stream.
   C. supercilia hair.
   D. cowlick. ___

6. Reggie's circular growth at his crown is known as a:

   A. C-shaping.
   B. barba hair.
   C. whorl.
   D. lanugo hair. ___

---

7. Juanita has just learned that she passed her esthetician's licensing exam. In her excitement, little bumps have appeared on her skin. These bumps are caused by the contraction of her:

   A. arrector pili muscle.
   B. sebaceous glands.
   C. suderiferous glands.
   D. hair bulb. ___

SITUATION FOR ITEMS 8–10:

Hong, Kim, and Hien are best friends. Hong's hair is naturally very curly. Kim's hair is straight, while Hien's hair is naturally wavy.

8. A cross-sectional view of Kim's hair will show that it has a/an ______________ shape.

   A. almost flat
   B. triangular
   C. oval
   D. round ___

9. Hong's hair has a shape that is:

   A. almost flat.
   B. round.
   C. oval.
   D. diamond. ___

10. Hien's hair has a cross-sectional shape that is:

A. round.
B. oval.
C. flat.
D. triangular. ___

---

11. Mark is fearful of growing bald. To help prevent this, it is important that he keep the health and nourishment of his:

A. melanin.
B. sebaceous glands.
C. papilla.
D. keratin. ___

SITUATION FOR ITEMS 12–14:

You are chemically coloring Bridget's scalp hair. In order to be successful, the chemicals will have different effects on the layers of Bridget's hair shaft.

12. Which layer of the hair shaft will the chemicals raise?

A. cortex
B. medulla
C. cuticle
D. pith ___

13. In which layer is Bridget's natural hair color found?

A. marrow
B. medulla
C. cuticle
D. cortex ___

14. What is the technical name for the hair on Bridget's head?

A. capilli
B. cilia
C. barba
D. supercilia ___

---

15. Thi Pham, a businessman, would like you to cut his hair exactly as short as you cut it the last time. It has been two months since the last haircut. How much hair will you cut off?

A. one-half inch
B. one inch
C. one and one-half inches
D. two inches ___

16. Linnea lives in Minnesota, where the winters are cold. During February, she vacations in Florida, where it is hot and humid. While on vacation her hair becomes curlier and thicker than it was in Minnesota. Why?

   1. heat causes hair to expand
   2. heat causes hair to shrink
   3. humidity deepens the natural wave
   4. cold air causes hair to expand

   A. 1 and 2
   B. 1 and 3
   C. 2 and 3
   D. 3 and 4 ___

17. Your client is concerned that too many hairs are falling out of her head. You inform her that it is normal to lose the following number of hairs per day:

   A. 10–30.
   B. 30–50.
   C. 50–80.
   D. 100–150. ___

SITUATION FOR ITEMS 18–19:

Sang, an esthetician, applies facial makeup to her client after performing a facial. Included in her makeup application are mascara and eyebrow pencil.

18. What is the technical name of the hair on which she applied mascara?

   A. barba
   B. capilli
   C. supercilia
   D. cilia ___

19. Eyebrow pencil was applied to her client's hair that is technically known as:

   A. barba.
   B. capilli.
   C. supercilia.
   D. cilia. ___

SITUATION FOR ITEMS 20–22:

Your client has absolutely no coloring matter in his skin, eyes, or hair.

20. The technical name for this person is:

    A. albino.
    B. trichoptilosis.
    C. monilethrix.
    D. pediculosis. ____

21. This situation is due to an absence of:

    A. keratin.
    B. sebum.
    C. hirsuties.
    D. melanin. ____

22. Another term for loss of pigment is:

    A. canities.
    B. alopecia.
    C. hypertrichosis.
    D. monilethrix. ____

---

23. Your client has trichoptilosis. This means that he has:

    A. head lice.
    B. split ends.
    C. ringed hair.
    D. ringworm. ____

24. Lua has facial hair that she does not like. She has hair above her upper lip and hair in front of her ears. This hair is known as:

    1. trichoptilosis
    2. hypertrichosis
    3. canities
    4. hirsuties
    5. pityriasis

    A. 1 and 2
    B. 2 and 3
    C. 2 and 4
    D. 3 and 5 ____

SITUATION FOR ITEMS 25–26:

During the client consultation you are to analyze the qualities of your client's hair. You stretch her hair to help in your analysis.

25. This stretching of the hair is a check for the hair's:

    A. porosity.
    B. density.
    C. texture.
    D. elasticity. ___

26. If the hair is wet, it can be stretched to what percent of its length?

    A. 10%–40%
    B. 40%–50%
    C. 50%–75%
    D. 75%–100% ___

27. Stefano, your client, is experiencing an abnormal amount of hair loss. This is called:

    A. tinea.
    B. pityriasis.
    C. scabies.
    D. alopecia. ___

SITUATION FOR ITEMS 28–29:

While brushing Mike's hair you notice that he has pediculosis.

28. This is commonly called:

    A. baldness.
    B. gray hair.
    C. head lice.
    D. ingrown hair. ___

29. You are to:

    A. continue with the service.
    B. refuse to continue the service.
    C. use medicated shampoo.
    D. condition Mike's hair. ___

30. While performing a facial, you notice that your client has a condition called ringworm. Another name for this is:

A. tinea.
B. scabies.
C. pityriasis.
D. canities. ___

31. Why does Consuelo have extremely oily skin? Because she has:

A. overactive sebaceous glands.
B. overactive suderiferous glands.
C. underactive sebaceous glands.
D. overactive arector pili muscles. ___

32. The technical name for the fine, short hairs found on Desiree's facial cheeks is:

A. capilli.
B. supercilia.
C. barba.
D. lanugo. ___

SITUATION FOR ITEMS 33–35:

A group of four clients has just entered your salon. Yvette has black hair, Vicky is a redhead, Meg has brown hair, and Briana is a blonde.

33. Who has the most hairs on her head?

A. Yvette
B. Vicky
C. Meg
D. Briana ___

34. Who has the fewest hairs on her head?

A. Yvette
B. Vicky
C. Meg
D. Briana ___

35. Approximately how many hairs does Yvette have on her head?

A. 90,000
B. 108,000
C. 110,000
D. 140,000 ___

---

36. Willie Smith is almost 60 years old and his hair is turning gray. This condition is known as:

A. acquired canities.
B. pityriasis steatoides.
C. congenital canities.
D. pediculosis.

___

SITUATION FOR ITEMS 37–38:

Unfortunately, Hiram was in the salon when it burned to the ground. Hiram was severely injured in the fire. His skin and hair were badly burned. One year later, some of his scalp hairs have started to grow, while some have not. His doctor has informed him that some of his scalp hairs will never grow again. However, all of his eyebrows and eyelashes have grown back.

37. Why will some of Hiram's scalp hairs never grow again?

A. the melanocytes were injured
B. because Hiram had canities
C. the papillas were destroyed
D. because Hiram acquired monilethrix

___

38. How long did it take for Hiram's eyelashes and eyebrows to be replaced?

A. 1–2 months
B. 4–5 months
C. 9–12 months
D. 1 year

___

SITUATION FOR ITEMS 39–41:

Ngoc's natural hair color is black. When it is shampooed, her hair does not absorb moisture very well and the water runs off.

39. The color of Ngoc's hair is determined by her:

A. keratin.
B. cold shaft.
C. elasticity.
D. melanin.

___

40. In which layer of Ngoc's hair is the coloring matter, or pigment, found?

    A. cortex
    B. medulla
    C. hypodermis
    D. cuticle ___

41. The resistance of her hair to absorb moisture refers to her hair's:

    A. elasticity.
    B. density.
    C. porosity.
    D. texture. ___

---

42. While combing your client's hair, you notice beads, or nodes, along the hair shaft. Some of the hair has already broken between these beads. The technical term for this condition is:

    A. trichorrhexis nodosa.
    B. hypertrichosis.
    C. trichoptilosis.
    D. monilethrix. ___

SITUATION FOR ITEMS 43–45:

Two of your regular clients, Chuck and Shari, have recently acquired dandruff. Chuck's dandruff is dry with little white scales. Shari's dandruff is greasy, waxy scales that stick to her scalp.

43. Chuck's type of dandruff is:

    A. pityriasis capitis simplex.
    B. pityriasis steatoides.
    C. alopecia areata.
    D. tinea capitis. ___

44. Shari's type of dandruff is:

    A. pityriasis capitis simplex.
    B. pityriasis steatoides.
    C. alopecia areata.
    D. tinea capitis. ___

45. Dandruff is considered to be:

    A. permanent.
    B. another form of pediculosis.
    C. contagious.
    D. noncontagious. ___

---

46. Ricardo has a boil on his skin. Another name for this is:

A. carbuncle.
B. scabies.
C. furuncle.
D. tinea.

___

47. Dung's hair and scalp get oily very quickly. Carla's hair and scalp are very dry. What is the substance that determines their oiliness or dryness?

A. melanin
B. keratin
C. hair bulb
D. sebum

___

SITUATION FOR ITEMS 48–49:

Two clients have arrived at your salon to have their hair cut. Chandra's hair is very fine. Hoang's hair is coarse.

48. "Fine" or "coarse" refers to the hair's:

A. texture.
B. density.
C. elasticity.
D. porosity.

___

49. The "fineness" or "coarseness" is determined by the hair's:

A. shape.
B. diameter.
C. length.
D. stretch.

___

---

50. Anthea has recently been extremely sick. Because of her illness, she now has round patches, or spots, of baldness. This condition is called alopecia:

A. senilis.
B. universal.
C. areata.
D. prematura.

___

5. Draping

SITUATION FOR ITEMS 1–5:

Bao is your haircutting client. Before cutting his hair, you will have a consultation, drape him, and shampoo his hair.

1. Which of the following are you to do before draping Bao?
   1. turn his collar to the inside
   2. prepare needed supplies
   3. sanitize Bao's hands
   4. remove your necklace
   5. sanitize your hands
   6. remove Bao's shoes

   A. 1, 2, and 5
   B. 1, 3, and 6
   C. 2, 4, and 5
   D. 3, 4, and 6 ___

2. In order to protect Bao during the haircut, you drape him with a cape and:

   A. towel.
   B. cotton coil.
   C. paper towel.
   D. neck strip. ___

3. Why are you to drape Bao during his haircut? To protect:
   1. your skin
   2. your clothing
   3. his skin
   4. his clothing

   A. 1 and 2
   B. 1 and 3
   C. 2 and 4
   D. 3 and 4 ___

4. The skin on Bao's neck should never come in contact with:

   A. the cape.
   B. the towel.
   C. the neck strip.
   D. your hands. ___

5. While cutting Bao's hair, you should use a/an ________ cape.

   A. comb-out
   B. shampoo
   C. cotton
   D. absorbent ___

SITUATION FOR ITEMS 6–8:

Hiroko is in your salon today for a haircut, perm, and facial.

6. While her hair has the perm chemicals on it, Hiroko's neck is to be draped with a cape and:

   A. cotton.
   B. neck strip.
   C. towel.
   D. paper towel. ___

7. Which of the following should you put around Hiroko's hairline before applying the chemicals to the hair?

   1. cotton coil
   2. alcohol
   3. 3% hydrogen peroxide
   4. protective cream

   A. 1 and 2
   B. 1 and 4
   C. 2 and 3
   D. 3 and 4 ___

8. Which of the following should be covered/protected while you give Hiroko a facial? Her:

   A. hair and legs.
   B. face and chest.
   C. hair and chest.
   D. chest and legs. ___

9. What type of cape should you use on Edna when you comb out her roller set?

   A. shampoo cape
   B. roller cape
   C. cotton cape
   D. comb-out cape ____

10. In a salon, you are to drape every client on whom you perform cosmetology services. Draping is for the protection of the:

    A. cosmetologist.
    B. client.
    C. salon owner.
    D. receptionist. ____

6. Shampooing, Rinsing, and Conditioning

SITUATION FOR ITEMS 1–5:

Travis has very oily hair. Ginny has an extremely dry scalp and hair. She is going to get a chemical hair relaxer today. Giovanni's hair is normal, but his scalp is irritated.

1. Who should shampoo his or her hair more often?

   A. Travis
   B. Ginny
   C. Giovanni
   D. they should all shampoo every day ___

2. Whose hair and scalp can be thoroughly brushed today?

   A. Giovanni's
   B. Ginny's
   C. Travis'
   D. all of the above ___

3. If Ginny's hair is extremely dry, you should:

   A. massage the scalp before relaxing the hair.
   B. condition the hair before relaxing it at a later date.
   C. use super strength relaxer.
   D. thoroughly brush the scalp before relaxing the hair. ___

4. After cutting Giovanni's hair, he asks you if it would be possible to get a bleach retouch today. You are to:

   A. dry his hair then bleach it.
   B. only bleach the new growth.
   C. re-wet his hair, then bleach it.
   D. refuse the service. ___

5. What do you suggest that Ginny have in the future in order to improve her condition?
   A. use a shampoo for lightened hair
   B. receive hard water rinses
   C. receive scalp treatments
   D. use a harsher shampoo ___

---

6. While vacationing in Oregon, Jane notices that her shampoo lathers a lot more than when she is in New York. This is because the water she is using in Oregon is:
   A. soft.
   B. hard.
   C. full of minerals.
   D. salt water. ___

7. Anne's Styling Salon's dispensary contains both water and hydrogen peroxide. What is the chemical symbol for water?
   A. HO
   B. H_2O
   C. H_2O_2
   D. H_3O_2 ___

8. Which of the following are you to do before wetting Dai's hair for a shampoo?
   1. wash his hands
   2. drape him
   3. apply the shampoo
   4. brush his hair
   5. wash your hands

   A. 1, 2, and 4
   B. 2, 3, and 4
   C. 2, 4, and 5
   D. 3, 4, and 5 ___

SITUATION FOR ITEMS 9–10:

Another cosmetologist has turned on the water at his shampoo bowl while you are rinsing your client's hair at your shampoo bowl.

9. This may cause changes in:
   1. water pressure
   2. cleanliness of the water
   3. water hardness
   4. water temperature

   A. 1 and 4
   B. 2 and 4
   C. 3 only
   D. 4 only ___

10. One of your fingers should be over the nozzle's edge so that you can monitor:

    A. the porosity.
    B. the client's action.
    C. when/if the hair has been thoroughly rinsed.
    D. the water temperature. ___

11. Livia's Salon uses shampoo that is acid-balanced. This means that this particular shampoo has a pH range of:

    A. 2.5–3.5
    B. 4.5–5.5
    C. 7.0–8.5
    D. 9.5–14.0 ___

12. Hope's mother fell down and has two broken legs. She is unable to get out of bed. What type of shampoo should Hope use on her mother's hair? A ____________ shampoo.

    A. medicated
    B. conditioning
    C. nonstrip
    D. dry ___

13. Chin has pityriasis capitis simplex. What type of shampoo should Chin use?

    A. medicated
    B. conditioning
    C. nonstrip
    D. dry ___

14. Manuel's Cosmetology Salon uses three different shampoos on their clients. Brand X has a pH of 5.5; brand Y has a pH of 7.0; brand Z has a pH of 13.5. Which of these shampoos is the harshest on the hair?

    A. brand X
    B. brand Y
    C. brand Z
    D. there is no difference between them ___

15. You have just completed lightening and toning Trish's hair. What type of rinse should you use on her hair? A/an ____________ rinse.

    A. color
    B. acid-balanced
    C. medicated
    D. cream ___

16. Nga's 4-year-old daughter has long hair. It tangles whenever Nga shampoos it. What can Nga use to make the tangled hair easier to comb? A/an __________ rinse.

    A. medicated
    B. color
    C. cream
    D. acid-balanced ___

17. The shampoo you are using has a pH of 6.5. On a pH scale, this would be a/an:

    A. protein.
    B. alkaline.
    C. neutral.
    D. acid. ___

18. Which of the following will temporarily darken Olaf's blond hair? A:

    A. nonstrip shampoo.
    B. color rinse.
    C. conditioning shampoo.
    D. temporary hair conditioner. ___

19. Mai has canities. What type of shampoo should you use on her? A ___________ shampoo.

    A. normal
    B. medicated
    C. dry
    D. highlighting ___

20. It is important to shampoo each client thoroughly. Failure to cleanse the scalp and hair regularly may lead to:

    A. canities.
    B. lanugo.
    C. scalp disorders.
    D. supercilia.

____

7. Haircutting

1. When choosing a style for Vera, it is important that you consider her:

   A. clothing color.
   B. physical coordination.
   C. finger dexterity.
   D. personality and lifestyle. ___

2. Jessie has very long hair. You are going to cut off eight inches. All of the following implements can remove hair length **EXCEPT**:

   A. razor.
   B. scissors.
   C. thinning shears.
   D. clipper. ___

SITUATION FOR ITEMS 3–8:

Your client has many coarse hairs on her head, and her hair looks too full for her face and is difficult to style. To improve this situation, you decide to remove excess bulk from her hair.

3. What is it called when you remove excess bulk without shortening the hair's length?

   A. spiking
   B. thinning
   C. effleurage
   D. blunt cutting ___

4. The amount of hair your client has on her head refers to her hair's:

   A. density.
   B. elasticity.
   C. texture.
   D. porosity. ___

5. If you decide to use a razor to remove the excessive bulk, the hair must be:

   A. dry.
   B. wet.
   C. conditioned.
   D. permed. ___

6. If you would rather use a thinning shear to remove the bulk, the hair:

   A. must be wet.
   B. must be at least 12 inches long.
   C. can be wet or dry.
   D. must be dry. ___

7. When you use scissors to remove the excess bulk, it is called:
   1. slithering.
   2. effilating.
   3. club cutting.
   4. effleurage.

   A. 1 and 2
   B. 1 and 4
   C. 2 and 3
   D. 3 and 4 ___

8. How far away from this client's scalp would you begin removing the excessive bulk? __________ inches.

   A. ½ to 1
   B. 1 to 1½
   C. 1½ to 2
   D. 2 to 3 ___

---

9. Spencer wants his hair to be dry when you cut it. What order should you follow?
   1. wash it
   2. cut it
   3. dry it
   4. drape him

   A. 4, 1, 2, 3
   B. 4, 1, 3, 2
   C. 4, 2, 3, 1
   D. 2, 4, 1, 3 ___

10. You have just cut the bottom length along your client's neck. This is the first section of hair that you have cut. This bottom length is also called:

    A. occipital bone.
    B. slithered hair.
    C. layered hair.
    D. the guide. ___

11. Mia would like her hair cut short at the nape and gradually longer at the crown without a definite line. In other words, Mia wants her hair:

    A. shingled.
    B. cut bluntly.
    C. slithered.
    D. effilated. ___

12. You have just finished cutting Andrea's hair. Before you begin perming it, you should:

    A. thoroughly brush her scalp.
    B. shampoo her hair again.
    C. apply a color rinse to her hair.
    D. clean up and discard the cut hair. ___

13. While shampooing your client before a haircut, you notice that he has alopecia. You are to:

    A. discontinue the service.
    B. have him sign a release form before continuing.
    C. suggest he see a physician.
    D. continue with the service. ___

14. Doan wants a razor cut. While cutting his hair, the razor's safety guard is to:

    A. face toward the cosmetologist.
    B. face away from the cosmetologist.
    C. be removed from the razor.
    D. used only if the blade is old. ___

15. Tina is a black woman and has a dry scalp. Before cutting her hair, you shampoo, thoroughly dry her hair, and apply:

    A. an antiseptic to her scalp.
    B. hydrogen peroxide to her hair.
    C. an emollient to her scalp.
    D. a color rinse to her hair. ___

SITUATION FOR ITEMS 16–18:

While cutting your client's hair, you notice that she has pediculosis.

16. What should you do?

    A. continue with the service
    B. refuse to continue with the service
    C. apply a disinfectant to the area
    D. suggest she color her hair ___

17. The common name for this condition is:

    A. athlete's foot.
    B. gray hair.
    C. hair loss.
    D. head lice. ___

18. This condition is to be treated by a:

    A. podiatrist.
    B. physician.
    C. cosmetologist.
    D. hair color technician. ___

---

19. For Rocco to be holding his haircutting scissors correctly, his third, or ring, finger should be:

    A. in the ring of the still blade.
    B. on the finger brace/tong.
    C. in the ring of the movable blade.
    D. not touching the scissors. ___

20. Sophia is using her thinning shears on her client's hair. The blades on this implement differ from a haircutting scissor in that they:

    A. are sharper.
    B. are notched.
    C. have replacement blades.
    D. are made of steel. ___

SITUATION FOR ITEMS 21–22:

Ted has short, very curly hair. You, the cosmetologist, give Ted a haircut using your electric clipper.

21. While cutting his hair, your clipper begins to pull Ted's hair. You are to:

    A. dry Ted's hair.
    B. apply water to your clipper.
    C. put oil on Ted's hair.
    D. apply oil to your clipper. ___

22. After completing the haircut on Ted, what do you use to sanitize your clipper?

    A. alcohol
    B. quaternary ammonium compounds
    C. sodium hypochlorite
    D. a germicidal solution ___

23. Tatsu has a haircut that he really likes. It is four inches longer on one side than it is on the other. This haircut is called:

    A. blended.
    B. asymmetrical.
    C. clockwise.
    D. symmetrical. ___

SITUATION FOR ITEMS 24–25:

It is a very busy day in the salon. One cosmetologist is an hour and a half behind schedule. The client in the chair wants a razor haircut. The client shampooed her own hair 3 hours ago. To save time, the cosmetologist decided not to shampoo the hair and to cut the hair dry. Later, when sanitizing implements, the cosmetologist discovered that her razor blade was dull.

24. What did the cosmetologist do wrong? She:

    A. razor cut the dry hair.
    B. was on time for the appointment.
    C. did not shampoo the hair.
    D. cut the hair 3 hours after it was shampooed. ___

25. What caused the razor blade to become dull?

    A. it was not sanitized right away
    B. it was used on wet hair
    C. it was used on dry hair
    D. the safety guard was not used ___

8. Finger Waving

SITUATION FOR ITEMS 1–3:

In some salons across the country, there are very few clients who request finger waves. Yet it is still a requirement for students to learn. Petra is a cosmetology instructor who teaches finger waves.

1. As cosmetology students learn how to finger wave, they also learn techniques of:

   1. moving the hair
   2. directing hair
   3. cutting hair
   4. cleansing the hair

   A. 1 and 2
   B. 1 and 3
   C. 2 and 3
   D. 3 and 4 ___

2. Petra's class is very important because her students will be developing their:

   A. hair shaping skills.
   B. finger dexterity.
   C. understanding of hair coloring.
   D. sanitation techniques. ___

3. During her lecture on finger waves, Petra informs her students that finger waves are:

   A. always in a clockwise direction.
   B. alternate, parallel waves.
   C. performed on dry hair.
   D. always vertical in their direction. ___

4. Sharon's fine hair has a natural wave; Chan has straight coarse hair; Cherie's hair has been pressed. Which of these will be easier to finger wave?

   A. Sharon
   B. Chan
   C. Cherie
   D. all of them would easily finger wave ___

5. Muriel wants waves in her hair that are weak with low ridges. These are called ____________ waves.

   A. horizontal
   B. prominent
   C. shadow
   D. vertical ___

6. The waving lotion that Quang uses on his clients should:

   A. take a long time to dry.
   B. color his client's hair.
   C. permanently curl their hair.
   D. be harmless to their hair. ___

7. While finger waving your client's hair, it will be easier for you and the waves will last longer if you:

   A. work against the natural hair growth.
   B. start at a closed end of the waves.
   C. follow the natural direction of hair growth.
   D. do not comb through to the scalp. ___

8. When should Rick apply the wave lotion to his client's hair?

   A. when it is dry
   B. before he shampoos it
   C. after finger waving it
   D. while it is still damp ___

9. Before placing her finger waving client under the hair dryer, Kristina is to:

   1. comb out the finger waves.
   2. set the dryer to a cool temperature.
   3. place a net over the hair.
   4. protect the client's ears.

   A. 1 and 2
   B. 1 and 3
   C. 3 and 4
   D. 2 and 4 ___

10. After the client's hair is dry, keeping the person under the dryer for a longer period of time will cause:

A. stronger finger waves.
B. weaker finger waves.
C. monilethrix to appear.
D. a dry condition of the scalp and hair. ____

9. Wet Hairstyling

1. Your shampoo and set client has just arrived at your salon. Before shampooing the hair you:

   A. remove the tangles from the hair.
   B. condition the hair.
   C. section the hair into five panels.
   D. blow the hair dry. ___

2. Diane is placing pin curls directly on the base of the curl. What type of stem is she using?

   A. no-stem
   B. quarter-stem
   C. half-stem
   D. full-stem ___

3. Vic is pin curling Mrs. Chan's hair. He is placing the hair ends outside of the curl/circle. What type of wave will he achieve by doing this?

   A. tighter curl toward the ends
   B. wider curl toward the ends
   C. wider curl at the scalp
   D. even curl throughout the strand ___

4. Leta wants her hair set with pin curls rather than rollers. She also wants the finished hairstyle to have a lot of mobility, or movement. You should set her hair in pin curls that are:

   A. no-stem.
   B. quarter-stem.
   C. half-stem.
   D. full-stem. ___

5. Your client would like her hair styled away from her face. In order to achieve this, the type of setting direction should be:

   A. forward.
   B. reverse.
   C. clockwise.
   D. counterclockwise. ____

6. Before Thaun sets his client's hair, he molds a section of her hair into a design. This section is his base for the curl formation, and is called a:

   A. curl.
   B. slice.
   C. shaping.
   D. part. ____

7. When Tim sets Mrs. Smith's hair in pin curls, he does not get splits along the front hairline. The reason for this is that Tim only uses bases that have a __________ shape.

   A. rectangular
   B. triangular
   C. half-moon
   D. square ____

SITUATION FOR ITEMS 8–10:

It is the day before a holiday, and Jeff is booked solid all day with clients who want their hair styled. When setting a client's hair on yellow rollers, Jeff realizes that he does not have enough sanitary yellow rollers to complete the set.

8. If Jeff chooses to use a roller with a smaller diameter than his yellow rollers, how will it effect the roller set? The hair on the smaller diameter roller will be:

   A. looser.
   B. curlier.
   C. straight.
   D. no difference in the curl. ____

9. If Jeff uses rollers that have a larger diameter than the yellow rollers, it will result in curls that are:

   A. looser.
   B. curlier.
   C. tighter.
   D. no difference in the curl. ____

10. If Jeff wants his client's curls to all be the same size, he can use any of the following **EXCEPT**:

A. stand-up curls the size of his yellow rollers.
B. a yellow roller as a guide to create rollerless, barrel curls.
C. cascade curls the size of his yellow rollers.
D. his unsanitized yellow rollers. ___

---

11. When setting her client's hair, Ngoc is alternating one row of finger waving with a second row of pin curls. She completes the entire head this way, alternating the direction of each row. Ngoc is performing:

A. cascade curls.
B. ridge curls.
C. skip waves.
D. stand-up waves. ___

12. Your client has long, straight hair. The person would like it set on rollers, but is afraid of achieving too much height or volume. In order to please this client, you should set the hair:

A. on base.
B. quarter on base.
C. half off base.
D. completely off base. ___

SITUATION FOR ITEMS 13–16:

Bruce is setting Ms. Dodd's hair with rollers that have one diameter at one end and a smaller diameter at the other end.

13. This type of roller is called:

1. mesh
2. tapered
3. magnetic
4. cylinder
5. sponge

A. 1 only
B. 2 and 3
C. 2 and 4
D. 3 and 5 ___

14. To use these rollers, Bruce must subsection Ms. Dodd's hair into a shape that is:

    A. rectangular.
    B. pie.
    C. square.
    D. oblong. ___

15. Which of the following is true concerning the amount of curl he will get?

    A. the hair on the small end will be looser
    B. the hair on the large end will be tighter
    C. the hair on the small end will be tighter
    D. there will be no difference in the curl ___

16. After Ms. Dodd's hair is completely dry, it is ready to be styled. After Bruce removes the rollers, and before he back-combs it, the hair should be:

    A. brushed.
    B. back-brushed.
    C. smoothed.
    D. dampened. ___

---

17. In order to achieve the small amount of height that she wants, Bernatta's hairstylist uses a technique called "ruffing." Another name for this is:

    A. effilating.
    B. tapering.
    C. slithering.
    D. back-brushing. ___

18. Jasmine is putting corn rows in her client's hair. Some people refer to this as a visible French braid. Regardless of the name used, Jasmine will achieve the look she wants if she plaits each strand:

    A. over.
    B. under.
    C. across.
    D. outward. ___

SITUATION FOR ITEMS 19–24:

Four clients have just entered the salon. Mohammed has a narrow forehead and a very wide jaw and chin. Lily has a heart-shaped face. The forehead and chin on Peter are narrow, while his cheekbones are wide. Hoang has an oval-shaped face.

19. What is Mohammed's facial shape?

    A. square
    B. heart
    C. pear
    D. oblong ___

20. How should Mohammed's hair be styled? With:

    A. no bangs; styled close to his head.
    B. fullness on the sides of his head.
    C. fullness along the jawline and no bangs.
    D. fullness and height; a soft fringe on the forehead. ___

21. Who has the ideal facial shape?

    A. Mohammed
    B. Lily
    C. Peter
    D. Hoang ___

22. How should Lily's hair be styled? With:

    A. fullness on top with no bangs.
    B. softness at the jaw and along the sides of the forehead.
    C. her ears exposed.
    D. fullness along the top and at the temples. ___

23. What is Peter's facial shape?

    A. diamond
    B. square
    C. pear
    D. oval ___

24. Peter's hair should be styled:

    A. close at the forehead and full at the cheeks.
    B. close at the sides with fullness at the forehead.
    C. with fullness at the nape, and close at the forehead.
    D. close at the sides and at the forehead. ___

25. Olivia has a large, prominent nose. To draw attention away from this, her hair should be styled:

    A. away from her face.
    B. with fullness at the occipital bone.
    C. with softness towards her face.
    D. past her chin in length. ____

SITUATION FOR ITEMS 26–27:

Sang has two regular clients that he sets using pin curls. Yen likes her hair very curly. Judy, on the other hand, prefers her hair looser than Yen's.

26. Which part of a pin curl determines this difference in curl size?

    A. base
    B. stem
    C. circle
    D. shaping ____

27. In order to please both clients, which of the following should Sang do?

    A. use a smaller circle on Yen
    B. use a smaller circle on Judy
    C. use long-stems on Yen and no-stems on Judy
    D. use square bases on Yen and triangular bases on Judy ____

---

28. Kate is setting the right, front hair toward her client's face. In what direction is she setting the hair?

    A. in a reverse movement
    B. clockwise
    C. backward
    D. counterclockwise ____

29. Loretta has placed shapings in her client's hair. Without disturbing the shapings, she is now carefully removing strands and pin curling them. Another name for this is type of curl is a ____________ curl.

    A. barrel
    B. carved
    C. cascade
    D. stand-up ____

SITUATION FOR ITEMS 30–31:

Claudia is going to a party tonight. She wants her hair to be as full and high as it can be.

30. To achieve this, the cosmetologist should set her hair ______________ base.

    A. off
    B. half off
    C. quarter on
    D. on ___

31. Additional fullness can be given to Claudia's hair by using:

    A. clockwise curls.
    B. large, tapered rollers.
    C. back-combing.
    D. vertical pin curls. ___

32. Which bonds break when Colleen's wet hair is set on rollers?

    A. salt
    B. hydrogen
    C. disulfide
    D. cystine ___

33. When selecting a new hairstyle for his client, Don should take into consideration all of the following **EXCEPT** the client's:

    A. profile.
    B. hair color.
    C. head shape.
    D. individual facial features. ___

10. Thermal Hairstyling

1. In Nikko's home, she has a thermostat and a thermometer. Each day, she brings a thermos bottle of coffee to her salon. In her salon, she has thermal irons. The word *thermal* refers to:

   A. electricity.
   B. power.
   C. heat.
   D. a fuel source. ___

2. Abdul has very coarse hair. The temperature of the irons used on his hair should be:

   A. cool.
   B. lukewarm.
   C. warm.
   D. hot. ___

3. Stacy's curling irons have a buildup of hairspray on them. To remove this, she should use:

   A. oil.
   B. an ammonia solution.
   C. 7% alcohol.
   D. an antiseptic. ___

4. What should Margaret place between her curling iron and her client's scalp in order to prevent skin burns?

   A. oil or cream
   B. a comb
   C. her fingers
   D. paper towels ___

5. Parnell is setting his station up for his thermal waving client. In doing this, he gathers together all of the following items **EXCEPT** his:

   A. thermal stove.
   B. combs.
   C. curling irons.
   D. waving lotion. ___

SITUATION FOR ITEMS 6–8:

Michelle's client has short, straight hair. After shampooing, Michelle blows it completely dry. She then proceeds to curl it using a large-barrel curling iron. As she gathers subsections of hair, some hairs are pulled tightly into the iron, while other hairs are loose and fall out of the iron. Upon completion, the client is unsatisfied because the hair is not very curly.

6. What could Michelle have done differently to make the hair curlier?

   A. used a larger-barrel curling iron
   B. used larger subsections
   C. used a smaller-barrel curling iron
   D. curled the hair with the iron when the hair was wet ___

7. Compared with the hairs that were loose and fell out of the iron, the hairs that were pulled tightly into the iron:

   A. were straighter.
   B. had less tension.
   C. were curlier.
   D. had no curl at all. ___

8. To prevent these short hairs from falling out, Michelle could also have:

   A. used smaller subsections.
   B. loosened her grip on the iron.
   C. used less tension.
   D. used an excessively hot iron. ___

---

9. After completing a curl with an iron, how should a hairstylist remove the iron from the hair?

   A. completely unwind the curl
   B. pull the iron 90 degrees out from the head
   C. slide the iron toward the iron's handles
   D. turn the iron tighter toward the scalp ___

10. Phong is using his curling iron and comb on his client's hair. The comb he uses should be made of:

A. plastic.
B. metal.
C. celluloid.
D. hard rubber. ___

11. Pam has long hair. Her cosmetologist curls it vertically with her curling iron. This is known as a/an ________________ curl.

A. croquignole
B. spiral
C. end
D. root ___

SITUATION FOR ITEMS 12–16:

It is the end of the day and Charlitta is cleaning her equipment and station area. Charlitta styled three clients with thermal irons today. She used off-base curls on Mara's long hair. Hoang's style had maximum amount of height and/or volume with a lot of curl. The third client, Angie, left with her short hair styled smoothly with little curl.

12. What type of base did Charlitta use on Hoang's hair?

A. on-base
B. quarter-base
C. half-base
D. off-base ___

13. Mara's hairstyle contained:

A. little volume.
B. a lot of curl.
C. maximum volume.
D. too much curl. ___

14. If Angie had wanted her hair curlier, what could Charlitta have done? Used:

A. a larger-barrel iron.
B. larger subsections.
C. a smaller-barrel iron.
D. off-base curls. ___

15. How often should Charlitta sanitize her thermal irons?

A. once a day
B. after each client
C. once a week
D. after use on three clients ___

16. Which of the following should she use to sanitize her irons?

A. a disinfectant solution
B. a dry sanitizer
C. an antiseptic solution
D. alcohol ___

---

17. Nam is afraid that his thermal iron is too hot and that it may burn his client's hair. Before using it on the hair, Nam is to test the temperature:

A. by splashing water on the iron.
B. with his fingers.
C. by using a hot towel.
D. by using tissue paper. ___

18. Yolanda's hair is chemically straightened. What could happen if thermal irons are used on her hair?

A. her hair may become damaged
B. scalp burns could occur
C. her hair may revert to its original curliness
D. the hair may change color ___

19. Cindy's hair has been pressed with thermal irons/combs. What type of thermal iron should **NOT** be used on Cindy's pressed hair? A/an ________________ thermal iron.

A. stove-heating
B. electric
C. vaporizing
D. self-heating ___

20. Bob's hair was styled by blow-drying. When completed, Bob's scalp was burned. Of the following, which could have caused the burns on Bob's scalp?

A. the air was directed away from the scalp
B. the temperature was set too low
C. Bob's hair was too wet
D. the temperature was set too high ___

21. Dat is finger waving his client's hair without using the separate steps of setting and drying it. He is using a special tool to achieve waves. The name of this implement is:

A. blow dryer.
B. air waver.
C. thermal iron.
D. pressing comb. ___

22. Dawn has had her hair professionally lightened for 12 years. After cutting it, her hairstylist plans to use a blow dryer to style it. Before actually styling it, the hairstylist first towel-dried Dawn's hair. This drying was done because lightened, wet hair:

A. dries very fast.
B. stretches easily and could become damaged.
C. is not porous, therefore it resists styling.
D. has a fine texture. ___

23. When blow-drying Tyler's hair, the hairstylist should direct the flow of air:

A. toward Tyler's scalp.
B. at the ends of Tyler's hair.
C. away from Tyler's scalp.
D. ½ inch off of Tyler's scalp. ___

24. The cape that Quy uses on his clients when he performs thermal waves should be made out of:

A. cloth.
B. plastic.
C. vinyl.
D. metal. ___

25. While she is blow-drying her client's hair, Elaine's blow dryer begins to smoke. What should Elaine do?

A. keep using it
B. spray water on it
C. douse it in water
D. unplug it ___

11. Permanent Waving

1. Your client Ms. Lund has you tint her hair each month with an aniline derivative tint. She is in your salon today for a permanent wave. What type of perm should you select to use on her hair?

   A. normal
   B. resistant
   C. tinted
   D. fine ____

2. You are giving John a permanent wave. As you are wrapping his hair on rods, you notice he has scabies on his scalp. You are to:

   A. put a disinfectant on the scalp before continuing.
   B. stop the service and suggest that he see a physician.
   C. continue with the perm service.
   D. place him under a cool dryer before neutralizing. ____

3. Tyler is a regular client who receives haircuts and perms from you. He wants a perm, but does not want it as curly as the last one. You are to:

   A. use larger rods.
   B. use smaller rods.
   C. use stronger solution.
   D. section his hair differently. ____

4. What should you place around Mrs. Gray's hairline in order to prevent her sensitive skin from becoming irritated?

   A. a plastic bag
   B. a cotton strip
   C. a disinfectant solution
   D. perm solution ____

5. You used gray concave rods on Ms. Jones and gray straight rods on Mr. Burns. Which of the following statements is true concerning the difference in the curl they received?

   A. Mr. Burns's curl is tighter on the ends
   B. Ms. Jones's curl is looser on the ends
   C. Ms. Jones's curl is tighter on the ends
   D. Mr. Burns's curl is looser at the scalp ____

6. You have just completed saturating your client's hair with an acid wave. When does it start to process?

   A. immediately
   B. when the neutralizer is applied
   C. when you cover the rods with a plastic bag
   D. when heat is applied ____

7. Laura, a regular client of yours, comes to you for permanent haircolor services and permanent waves. She has been out of town for six weeks and needs both a color and a perm. You are to:

   A. color it today, and perm it tomorrow.
   B. perm it today, and color it in 7–10 days.
   C. color it today, and perm it in two weeks.
   D. perm it today, and color it tomorrow. ____

8. Jody has made an appointment with you for a perm. You have never done her hair before. During your consultation, you learn that Jody has been bleaching her own hair for 12 years and swims in her condominium's pool every night after work. You are to:

   A. perm it today.
   B. use a cream rinse, then perm it today.
   C. use a perm for resistant hair.
   D. get it in appropriate condition before perming it at a later date. ____

9. While sectioning Bob's hair for a perm, you notice he has canities. You are to:

   A. continue the perm procedure.
   B. apply an antiseptic to his scalp.
   C. discontinue the perm and suggest that he see a physician.
   D. use a perm for bleached hair. ____

10. You have just completed the sectioning, wrapping, and processing of a permanent wave on Ann's hair. In correct order, what are the next three steps that you do?

    A. towel blot, remove rods, neutralize
    B. remove rods, rinse, neutralize
    C. rinse, towel blot, neutralize
    D. rinse, remove rods, neutralize ____

11. David's hair is wrapped and ready for the application of the waving solution. Unexpectedly, a temporary power failure has all of your hair dryers not working. What type of perm can you use that does not require a hair dryer?

    A. alkaline
    B. acid
    C. piggyback
    D. spiral ____

12. Tom has never received a perm in his life and is quite nervous. During your consultation, you explain to him the physical and chemical processes of a perm in order to make him more comfortable. While discussing this, you inform him of the two chemical processes, which are:

    A. waving lotion and ammonia.
    B. neutralizer and sodium hydroxide.
    C. thioglycolate and an alkaline.
    D. waving lotion and neutralizer. ____

13. You have just received a shipment of perms into the salon. You have never used these particular perms before and are not quite sure how to use them. Whose directions do you follow?

    A. the salon manager's
    B. the manufacturer's
    C. your co-worker who has used them before
    D. your instructor's ____

14. The perm you are using requires that you mix two chemicals together for your waving lotion. You notice that as you mix these, the solution in the bottle gets warm. What is this type of perm called?

    A. alkaline
    B. acid
    C. ammonia-free
    D. exothermic ____

15. When perming Lisa's hair, there are two actions that are occurring. Wrapping the hair around a rod is considered to be a/an ______________ action.

    A. chemical
    B. oxidation
    C. physical
    D. processing

    ___

16. Neutralizing is a very important step in perming. What would happen if a person removed the rods, rinsed the hair, and completely forgot to apply the neutralizer? The hair would:

    A. be very curly.
    B. not be curly.
    C. change color.
    D. be unable to perm again.

    ___

17. Amy is a new perm client in your salon. Because of this, the client consultation with her must be very thorough. Which of the following is **NOT** to be considered in your consultation with Amy?

    A. her political views
    B. how much curl she wants
    C. her lifestyle
    D. her previous perming experiences

    ___

SITUATION FOR ITEMS 18–20:

As you shampoo Amy before her perm, you notice that her hair does not get wet very well. In fact, it seems that the water runs off of her hair.

18. This tells you that her hair is:

    A. very porous.
    B. not very elastic.
    C. fine.
    D. resistant.

    ___

19. Amy's processing time will most likely be:

    A. longer than average.
    B. average.
    C. shorter than average.
    D. not affected.

    ___

20. For Amy's hair type, you should choose a perm solution made for ______________ hair.

A. normal
B. resistant
C. fine
D. bleached
___

SITUATION FOR ITEMS 21–22:

During your consultation with your client Derek, you determine that his hair is very fine.

21. "Fine" refers to his hair's:

A. elasticity.
B. density.
C. texture.
D. porosity.
___

22. Compared with coarse hair, fine hair becomes saturated with waving lotion:

A. much slower.
B. more rapidly.
C. at the same speed.
D. less thoroughly.
___

---

23. To check a client's hair for its elasticity, the cosmetologist performs a ______________ test.

A. patch
B. match
C. predisposition
D. stretch
___

24. Amanda has very few hairs on her head. This refers to her hair's:

A. density.
B. porosity.
C. texture.
D. elasticity.
___

25. Preparing Amanda before her perm should include all of the following **EXCEPT**:

A. scalp and hair analysis.
B. draping.
C. vigorous brushing.
D. shampooing. ___

26. Betty wants a perm that is curlier than the one you gave her six months ago. Her client record card tells you that you used white rods last time. One choice you could make would be to use rods that are:

A. brown.
B. purple.
C. white.
D. gray. ___

27. What sectioning pattern should be used if your client wants the hair in the crown area smooth?

A. single halo
B. straight back
C. dropped crown
D. double horseshoe ___

28. Rita, a popular cosmetologist, folds her end papers to cover both sides of a strand of hair. What is the name of end wrap type that Rita uses? A ____________ ____________ wrap.

A. book end
B. double end
C. single end
D. double safety ___

29. Your perm client Crystal has extremely long hair—it extends far down her back. What type of perm should you give her?

A. roller
B. piggyback
C. root
D. cushion ___

30. A client comes to you for a perm. The person has bleached her own hair and plays tennis every day in the sun. Before perming this client's hair, it would be advisable to:

A. perform a preliminary test curl.
B. re-bleach the hair.
C. perform a match test.
D. perform a scalp massage. ___

31. The manufacturer's directions for a particular perm state that you are to take a test curl every 3–5 minutes. What do you look for when performing a test curl?

A. straight hair
B. slinky-shaped hair
C. a firm C-shaping
D. a firm S-shaping ___

32. Ms. Ross received a perm yesterday. She has stopped into your salon today and is complaining that the perm caused her hair to change color. What caused this to happen? The:

A. waving lotion was not on long enough.
B. hair was not shampooed first.
C. waving lotion was on too long.
D. hair was wrapped improperly. ___

33. Outside it is very hot and humid. A client has just entered your air-conditioned salon and first wants a haircut and then a permanent wave. You are to:

A. place the client under a hot dryer before the perm.
B. place the client under a cool dryer before the haircut.
C. cut the hair first, then perm it.
D. perm the hair first, then cut it. ___

34. Todd has all four of the following skin lesions on his scalp. Which of these **CANNOT** be permed?

A. pustule
B. scar
C. macule
D. verruca ___

35. While processing Cheryl's perm, you notice a pink-purple liquid dripping into the protective cotton. You are to:

A. reschedule the service.
B. continue with the service.
C. stop the service.
D. get medical attention. ___

36. Debra loved the last perm that you gave her. You check her record card from the last time. All of the following are to be on a client record **EXCEPT**:

A. date of last perm.
B. rod size.
C. particular perm used.
D. sanitation techniques. ___

37. As you check Monique's hair and scalp before giving her a perm, you notice she has pediculosis. You are to:

A. refuse to give her a service today.
B. continue with the perm.
C. give her a scalp treatment today and postpone the perm for one week.
D. apply protective cream to the areas with pediculosis. ___

38. Cy's perm is very curly when it is wet and frizzy when it is dry. The reason for this is that his perm was:

A. not sectioned properly.
B. underprocessed.
C. overprocessed.
D. not wrapped properly. ___

39. While you were giving Ethel a perm, some wave solution dripped into her eyes. You are to flush her eyes with:

A. cool water.
B. warm water.
C. hot water.
D. neutralizer. ___

40. You are in the middle of giving your client a perm. It is now the "processing time." What specific chemical is on the hair during this time?

A. sodium hydroxide
B. neutralizer
C. hydrogen peroxide
D. waving lotion ___

41. As you arrive at the salon, you notice you have three perms scheduled for today. Although these three people may require different rod sizes, processing times, and various brands of perms, the basic perm procedure will be the same. What is the correct procedure for a basic perm?

1. process
2. wrap the rods
3. neutralize
4. section/block

A. 4, 3, 2, 1
B. 4, 2, 1, 3
C. 1, 2, 4, 3
D. 3, 4, 1, 2 ___

SITUATION FOR ITEMS 42–43:

Mario wants support for his hairstyle without a lot of curl.

42. The type of perm Mario wants is called a/an ___________ wave.

    A. exothermic
    B. body
    C. alkaline
    D. acid-balanced ___

43. The difference between Mario's type of perm and a curly perm is determined by the:

    A. wrapping pattern.
    B. blocking method.
    C. end wrap method.
    D. size of the rod. ___

44. Peggy has just arrived for her perm appointment. She has an open sore on her scalp. You should:

    A. work very carefully around the sore.
    B. put protective cream on the sore and proceed with the service.
    C. reschedule the appointment for when the sore heals.
    D. ignore the sore and proceed with the perm. ___

45. Juan received a perm a month ago at another salon. While cutting his hair, you notice a lot of hair breakage from that perm. This breakage occurred because the:

    A. rods were wrapped too loosely.
    B. ends were wrapped too tightly.
    C. fastening device was too tight at the scalp.
    D. rod size was too small. ___

46. You have just completed giving a perm. The client is somewhat satisfied with the results, but wants her hair curlier the next time you perm it. This means that the next time, the rod size you use will:

    A. be larger in diameter.
    B. be smaller in diameter.
    C. be larger in length.
    D. be smaller in length. ___

47. Immediately after applying the waving lotion to your client's hair, a severe burning sensation on her entire scalp occurs. You:

A. immediately rinse the wave lotion off with water.
B. continue processing the perm.
C. spray the entire head with disinfectant spray.
D. wait at least five minutes, then neutralize the hair. ____

48. Karen's hair cannot be permed if she has colored it with a/an:

A. lightener/bleach.
B. aniline derivative tint.
C. color rinse.
D. metallic dye. ____

49. As you are wrapping Burt's hair, you use smaller rods in the nape area. As the rod size decreases, the subsection should:

A. increase.
B. decrease.
C. remain the same.
D. become wider. ____

50. Cotton that is wet with waving lotion has not been removed from Vince's hairline. This could cause:

A. curlier hair.
B. hair breakage.
C. skin irritation.
D. pediculosis. ____

12. Hair Coloring

SITUATION FOR ITEMS 1–4:

Mary's hair is too red. She wants to get rid of the red. To achieve this, her cosmetologist will apply a hair coloring product with a green base.

1. On the color wheel, red and green are ___________ colors.

   A. tertiary
   B. levels of
   C. complementary
   D. quaternary ___

2. Which of the following statements are true concerning the colors red and green?

   1. red is a secondary color
   2. green is a secondary color
   3. red is a primary color
   4. green is a primary color
   5. red is a tertiary color

   A. 1 and 4
   B. 2 and 3
   C. 3 and 4
   D. 4 and 5 ___

3. What will the green color do to Mary's red?

   A. enhance the red
   B. lighten the level of her hair
   C. neutralize the red
   D. add warm tones ___

4. Which of the following statements are true concerning the tones of red and green?
   1. red gives warm tones
   2. green gives warm tones
   3. red gives ash/drab tones
   4. green gives ash/drab tones

   A. 1 and 4
   B. 2 and 3
   C. 2 and 4
   D. 3 and 4 ___

---

5. What type of hair color is mascara, which is applied to a client's eyelashes?

   A. temporary
   B. semi-permanent
   C. permanent
   D. high-lift ___

SITUATION FOR ITEMS 6–10:

A cosmetologist is in the salon's dispensary mixing a permanent hair color for a client's hair. The client has not had her hair colored for 2 months. The client came to the salon yesterday and received a patch test.

6. What is the cosmetologist mixing with the hair color?

   A. H_2O
   B. H_2O_2
   C. H_2O_3
   D. H_2O_4 ___

7. Other names for permanent hair color include:
   1. aniline derivative tints
   2. vegetable tints
   3. penetrating tints
   4. synthetic-organic tints
   5. compound dyes

   A. 1 and 4
   B. 2 and 3
   C. 1, 3, and 5
   D. 1, 3, and 4 ___

8. How far from the scalp will this client's line of demarcation be?

   A. 6 inches
   B. 2 inches
   C. 1 inch
   D. at the scalp ___

9. If the stylist is going to color the client's hair, it means that the patch test results were:

   A. positive.
   B. negative.
   C. neutral.
   D. inconclusive. ___

10. A patch test is required for all hair coloring products that:

   A. are mixed with a developer.
   B. deposit into the cortex.
   C. have an alkaline pH.
   D. contain aniline derivative. ___

---

11. When performing a virgin tint going lighter, where on the client's hair do you first apply the color?

   A. 3 inches from the scalp
   B. 2 inches from the scalp
   C. 1 inch from the scalp
   D. at the scalp ___

SITUATION FOR ITEMS 12–13:

Thuy uses a hair color product that shampoos out in four to six shampoos.

12. The type of color product used on her hair is:

   A. temporary.
   B. semi-permanent.
   C. permanent.
   D. a compound dye. ___

13. All of the following are true about this type of hair color **EXCEPT:**

   A. it is mixed with hydrogen peroxide.
   B. a patch test is required if it contains aniline derivative.
   C. usually no retouching is required.
   D. Thuy's natural pigment is not changed. ___

---

14. A client has entered the salon for a tint retouch. The salon has run out of hydrogen peroxide. What should be done?

    A. mix the color with water
    B. use the color without hydrogen peroxide
    C. mix the color with acetone
    D. reschedule the appointment ___

15. When doing a tint retouch, the cosmetologist accidently spills the tint on the client's clothing. What should the cosmetologist do?

    A. ignore it and hope the client doesn't notice
    B. tell the client to wash it as soon as she gets home
    C. blame the client for moving her head around
    D. offer to pay the cleaning bill ___

16. Bill is highlighting his client's hair using the foil technique. What type of lightener is he using?

    A. powder
    B. cream
    C. liquid
    D. aniline ___

17. A client with naturally black hair comes to the salon to have her hair lightened to a pale blonde color. One of the first things you should do is:

    A. lighten it.
    B. explain how hard and damaging it would be.
    C. condition the hair.
    D. refuse to do the service. ___

SITUATION FOR ITEMS 18–24:

Linda's natural hair color is dark brown. During her consultation with her hair color technician, James, Linda decides that she would like her hair four shades lighter—a lighter brown color. James discusses with her the need for regular tint retouches in the future, and the upkeep involved in coloring her hair. James decides to use a high lift tint in order to get the color Linda wants. They proceed with the service and Linda is very happy with the results.

18. The type of application James performs is a:

    A. virgin tint lighter.
    B. virgin tint darker.
    C. tint retouch.
    D. lightener retouch. ___

19. The color that James uses contains:

    A. certified color/s.
    B. vegetable dyes.
    C. aniline derivative.
    D. metallic dyes. ___

20. How far from the scalp did James first apply the color?

    A. at the scalp
    B. 1 inch from the scalp
    C. 2 inches from the scalp
    D. 3 inches from the scalp ___

21. Into which layer of Linda's hair were the color molecules deposited?

    A. medulla
    B. epidermis
    C. cuticle
    D. cortex ___

22. In order to penetrate into the hair, the pH of a tint must be:

    A. acid.
    B. balanced.
    C. neutral.
    D. alkaline. ___

23. When Linda returns for a retouch in 4 to 6 weeks, where on the hair shaft will James first apply the color?

    A. at the scalp
    B. 1 inch from the scalp
    C. 2 inches from the scalp
    D. 3 inches from the scalp ___

24. In 4 to 6 weeks, how will James know which color/s he used on Linda's hair?

    A. he'll check his written patch test results
    B. Linda will tell him
    C. he'll check his client record card on Linda
    D. the client release form that Linda signed will tell him ___

25. The Beauty Nook Salon has many temporary rinses in its dispensary. A few of the rinses contain aniline derivative as an ingredient. What does this mean?

A. a strand test must be done
B. a patch test must be done
C. a match test must be done
D. no test is performed with these rinses ___

26. Heidi wants to be a cool blonde shade. Which of the following is a cool-based color?

A. red
B. gold
C. yellow
D. blue ___

27. Quang would like his gray hairs colored, but is afraid of any type of permanent hair coloring. He would like the color to shampoo out the next time he shampoos his hair. What type of hair coloring product should be used on Quang? A:

A. temporary color.
B. compound dye.
C. semi-permanent color.
D. metallic dye. ___

SITUATION FOR ITEMS 28–32:

Immediately before applying a permanent color to his client's hair, Richard mixes the color with hydrogen peroxide. His client tints her hair darker than her hair is naturally.

28. What strength of peroxide does Richard use?

A. 20-volume
B. 30-volume
C. 40-volume
D. 60-volume ___

29. What is the name of the chemical reaction that occurs when the hydrogen peroxide mixes with the color molecules?

A. contraction
B. melano-reactor
C. oxidation
D. development ___

30. The pH of stable hydrogen peroxide is:

A. 3.5–4.0.
B. 4.5–5.5.
C. 7.0.
D. 8.5–10.0. ___

31. If Richard wants his mixture to be easy to control and not to run or drip on the client, what type of peroxide should he use?

A. tablet
B. liquid
C. powder or dry
D. cream or gel ___

32. All of the following are other names for peroxide **EXCEPT**:

A. catalyst.
B. stabilizer.
C. developer.
D. oxidizer. ___

SITUATION FOR ITEMS 33–35:

Using a crochet hook, Suki is pulling strands of hair through a plastic covering on her client's head. She is then going to lighten just the hair strands that are on the outside of the plastic covering using the fastest and strongest type of hair lightener.

33. This highlighting technique is called:

A. the foil technique.
B. streaking.
C. the cap technique.
D. a soap cap. ___

34. What type of lightener did Suki use?

A. liquid
B. gel
C. powder
D. cream ___

35. What should Suki do if she drops her only crochet hook on the floor?

A. sanitize it with alcohol
B. pick it up and continue using it
C. immerse it in a disinfectant solution
D. wipe it off on a clean towel ___

SITUATION FOR ITEMS 36–37:

Your client has 4 inches of virgin, brown hair close to her scalp. She also has 6 inches of hair toward the ends that she has lightened to pale yellow. The last 3 inches of the lightened hair also have curl on them from an old perm. The client wants her hair colored as close to her natural color as possible.

36. The procedure that your client wants is known as a:

    A. tint-back.
    B. redo.
    C. virgin tint darker.
    D. single process. ___

37. What should first be applied to the hair? A:

    A. hair lacquer.
    B. color filler.
    C. dye solvent.
    D. color drabber. ___

SITUATION FOR ITEMS 38–39:

Two of your clients do not like their current hair color and want you to change it. Omar does not have any hair coloring product on his naturally dark brown hair. He would like it lighter. Isabelle's brown hair has been tinted red with a permanent color. She wants the red tint out of her hair.

38. Which of the following products will diffuse Omar's natural melanin? A:

    A. color filler.
    B. dye solvent.
    C. drabber.
    D. lightener. ___

39. Which of the following products will diffuse Isabelle's artificial color? A:

    A. color filler.
    B. dye solvent.
    C. drabber.
    D. polymer. ___

40. When coloring hair, which of the following do you use to protect the client? A:

    A. clean cape.
    B. paper neck strip and cape.
    C. base applied to the scalp.
    D. towel and cape. ___

41. Doan is getting his hair colored for the first time. The cosmetologist is applying permanent tint to each subsection from Doan's scalp to the ends. What type of color application is Doan receiving?

    A. virgin lightener (bleach)
    B. tint retouch darker
    C. virgin tint lighter
    D. virgin tint darker ___

42. This is the first time that Hien has come to your salon. She has been coloring her own hair for 10 years, and wants you to color it today. The first thing you do is:

    A. a strand test.
    B. a predisposition test.
    C. remove her current color.
    D. look for scalp abrasions. ___

SITUATION FOR ITEMS 43–50:

Ramona has naturally dark brown hair and would like to be a dark to medium blonde. In order to achieve this, her cosmetologist first lightens her hair, and then applies a blonde toner. Ramona loves her new look, and realizes that she must go back to the salon often to maintain her blonde color.

43. What type of color application was performed on Ramona's hair?

    A. foil highlighting
    B. highlighting
    C. single process
    D. double process ___

44. When rinsing lightener from Ramona's hair, the cosmetologist should use:

    A. a color rinse.
    B. cool water.
    C. hot water.
    D. a cream rinse. ___

45. Which hair coloring product required that a patch test be performed? The:

A. lightener.
B. hydrogen peroxide.
C. toner.
D. bleach. ___

46. What type of lightener did the cosmetologist use on Ramona's hair?

A. cream
B. speed
C. liquid
D. powder ___

47. Where is the lightener first applied to Ramona's hair?

A. at the ends
B. 2 inches from the scalp
C. 1 inch from the scalp
D. on the hot shaft ___

48. When is Ramona's hair able to accept a toner?

A. after it has been lightened
B. before it is shampooed
C. before any other chemicals are applied to it
D. after it is shampooed ___

49. When Ramona returns to the salon in a month, where will the cosmetologist first apply the lightener?

A. at the scalp
B. 1 inch from the scalp
C. 2 inches from the scalp
D. at the ends ___

50. What should the cosmetologist do if Ramona's scalp burns?

A. apply neutralizer
B. rinse the area with hot, soapy water
C. rinse her head with tepid water
D. rinse the area with cold water and shampoo her ___

13. Chemical Hair Relaxing and Soft Curl Permanent

SITUATION FOR ITEMS 1–6:

Rosa's hair is chemically relaxed. She has relaxed her hair with sodium hydroxide relaxers for the past 5 years. She is in the salon today to have it relaxed, as it has been 4 months since her last chemical service. Yoshanna, the hairstylist, is just beginning the relaxing service on Rosa.

1. Yoshanna will need all of the following products **EXCEPT**:

   A. curl booster.
   B. chemical relaxer.
   C. base cream.
   D. neutralizer. ____

2. What will the relaxer do to Rosa's hair?

   A. permanently reform the hair into a curly formation
   B. temporarily straighten Rosa's curly hair
   C. permanently straighten Rosa's curly hair
   D. temporarily press Rosa's hair ____

3. What type of relaxer should Yoshanna use on Rosa's hair?

   A. sodium bromate
   B. sodium hydroxide
   C. ammonium thioglycolate
   D. ammonium hydroxide ____

4. When will Rosa's hair be shampooed?

   A. before her hair is relaxed
   B. after her hair is relaxed
   C. after her hair is thoroughly brushed
   D. before the base is applied ____

5. Where on the hair shaft will Yoshanna apply the relaxer?

   A. 1 inch from the scalp
   B. from the scalp to the ends
   C. to the previously relaxed hair first, then to the new growth
   D. to the new growth only ___

6. What is the pH range of the type of relaxer used on Rosa's hair?

   A. 4.5–5.5
   B. 7.0
   C. 7.5–8.5
   D. 10–14 ___

---

7. Marshall has naturally over-curly hair. He does not want it straight, but he would like to remove some of his natural curl so that he can style it easily. Which of the following services should Marshall receive? A:

   A. virgin chemical relaxer.
   B. chemical relaxer retouch.
   C. chemical blow-out.
   D. soft curl permanent. ___

8. Monique has just arrived at the salon for her soft curl permanent appointment. During the consultation, the cosmetologist realizes that Moniques's hair is chemically relaxed. The cosmetologist is to:

   A. refuse the service.
   B. reschedule the appointment until next week.
   C. proceed with the soft curl permanent service.
   D. condition her hair before perming it. ___

9. What strength relaxer should be used on Pam's fine hair?

   A. extra
   B. super
   C. normal
   D. mild ___

SITUATION FOR ITEMS 10–13:

Christopher has a soft curl permanent on his hair. He has had this type of perm for the last 2 years. It has been 6 months since his last soft curl perm and he is in your salon today for another one. His friend Jesse is with him because he wants a perm like Christopher's. Jesse's sister has relaxed and colored Jesse's hair with a metallic dye.

10. The chemical in Christopher's soft curl perm is:

A. ammonium bromate.
B. ammonium thioglycolate.
C. sodium hydroxide.
D. sodium bromate. ___

11. Put the following in proper sequential order for Christopher's cosmetologist to follow.

1. wrap on rods
2. shampoo
3. neutralize
4. relax the new growth
5. process the curl

A. 2, 4, 1, 5, 3
B. 2, 3, 4, 5, 1
C. 3, 4, 1, 2, 5
D. 4, 1, 3, 5, 2 ___

12. What should the cosmetologist inform/tell Jesse concerning his hair? That he can:

A. get a soft curl perm today.
B. never get a soft curl perm.
C. get a soft curl perm with his sister's permission.
D. get a soft curl perm after the relaxer and color have been cut off. ___

13. While neutralizing the hair, the cosmetologist accidently gets neutralizer in Christopher's left eye. The cosmetologist should:

A. proceed with the service.
B. flush the eye with hot water.
C. flush the eye with cool water.
D. have Christopher rub his eye. ___

---

14. Your client has just entered the salon. This person is an athlete and has just jogged the 5 miles from home to your salon for a chemical relaxing service. You should:

A. start the service immediately.
B. refuse to do the service today.
C. use a different chemical than you had planned.
D. place the client under a cool dryer before relaxing the hair. ___

15. A woman with over-curly, virgin hair would like her hair permanently straightened. She is afraid of her hair getting chemically damaged. The cosmetologist chooses a relaxer with a low pH to use on this woman's hair. Which of the following chemicals is lowest in pH?

A. ammonium thioglycolate
B. sodium hydroxide
C. no-base relaxer
D. base relaxer ____

16. While you are applying a chemical relaxer, a chemical burn occurs on your client's skin. You are to:

A. apply neutralizer to the area.
B. apply cold water to the scalp.
C. wipe the area with a towel.
D. apply a disinfectant to the area with cotton. ____

17. In performing a soft curl permanent, what chemical is used to straighten the hair before it is curled?

A. sodium hydroxide
B. ammonium thioglycolate
C. sodium bromate
D. hydrogen peroxide ____

18. A client with permanently colored hair comes to you for a soft curl permanent. During the consultation and hair/scalp analysis, you notice hair breakage from previous chemicals. You:

A. proceed with the scheduled service.
B. only wrap on rods, process and neutralize the hair.
C. refuse the service and condition the hair.
D. condition the hair and then proceed with the scheduled perm today. ____

19. You have been giving soft curl perms to Debbie's hair for a long time. After performing another perm on her, the ends of her hair are straight. Why did this happen?

A. the chemical was left on too long
B. the new growth was not relaxed enough
C. her ends are damaged from previous chemicals
D. her ends were wrapped on small rods ____

20. Your client is in the salon to receieve a relaxer and a haircut. He has 3 inches of new growth, and then 6 inches of a soft curl perm toward the hair ends. You:

    A. cut the curl off and then relax the new growth.
    B. relax all of the hair.
    C. relax the new growth first, then the ends.
    D. press and curl the hair. ___

SITUATION FOR ITEMS 21–24:

A cosmetologist has just completed a relaxer retouch on Tenille's hair. She had 2 inches of new growth. The cosmetologist applied a no-base sodium hydroxide relaxer to the first 3 inches of hair in the scalp area. The hair was shampooed twice with the neutralizing shampoo—just as the directions state. A few days later, Tenille noticed her hair was breaking off and the cosmetologist's hands were chemically burned.

21. Tenille's hair breakage was caused by:

    A. underprocessing.
    B. overlapping.
    C. over neutralizing.
    D. insufficient coverage. ___

22. Why did the cosmetologist's hands get burned?

    A. too much pressure was used on the hair
    B. the relaxer strength was too strong
    C. the hair was shampooed two times
    D. gloves were not worn ___

23. The cosmetologist relaxed, rinsed, and shampooed Tenille's hair. What is the next step done to the hair?

    A. neutralize
    B. analyze
    C. condition
    D. set/style ___

24. A no-base relaxer was used on Tenille. This means that:

    A. base cream is not applied.
    B. base cream is applied.
    C. base cream comes with the relaxer kit.
    D. the relaxer product is very strong. ___

---

25. Which bonds are broken in Tony's hair when it is chemically permed or relaxed?

A. only the salt
B. the salt and hydrogen
C. only the hydrogen
D. the cystine disulfide and hydrogen ____

14. Thermal Hair Straightening (Hair Pressing)

SITUATION FOR ITEMS 1–4:

Karla's coarse hair is thermally straightened by her hairstylist. Each section of hair is pressed twice on each side. After pressing Karla's hair, her hairstylist needs to clean the pressing comb/s. After wiping any excess hair and grease off, it is rubbed with an emery board or a steel wool pad.

1. What type of press does Karla receive?

   A. soft
   B. medium
   C. hard
   D. permanent ___

2. The "coarseness" of Karla's hair refers to its:

   A. texture.
   B. density.
   C. elasticity.
   D. porosity. ___

3. Pressing coarse hair like Karla's usually requires:

   1. more heat
   2. less heat
   3. more pressure
   4. less pressure

   A. 1 only
   B. 2 only
   C. 1 and 3
   D. 1 and 4 ___

4. What does either the emery board or the steel wool pad remove from the pressing comb?

   A. shine
   B. carbon
   C. oxygen
   D. creosol

---

5. Pierre is preparing his client's hair for a press. When does he apply pressing oil to the hair?

   A. before it is shampooed
   B. before it is brushed
   C. after it has been pressed
   D. after it has been dried

6. Ramon is half-way done pressing his client's hair. He is concerned because the hair is smoking. What could be the cause of this smoke?

   A. the hair is too wet
   B. the hair was not shampooed first
   C. Ramon applied too much oil to the hair
   D. Ramon's iron is too cool

SITUATION FOR ITEMS 7–12:

Two clients are in the salon for thermal straightening services. Carl's short hair is fine, and Isianita's hair is long and coarse. The cosmetologist presses Carl's hair once on each side. Isianita's hair is pressed twice on each side and her scalp on the back of her head is burned.

7. How long will Isianita's hair stay pressed?

   A. permanently
   B. until it is shampooed
   C. semi-permanently
   D. one week

8. How hot should the combs be for pressing Carl's hair?

   A. very hot
   B. 98.6 degrees Fahrenheit
   C. hotter than the combs used on Isianita
   D. cooler than the combs used on Isianita

9. Before pressing Isianita's hair, the cosmetologist should test the comb's temperature by using:

   A. white paper.
   B. her fingers.
   C. a plastic cape.
   D. a strand test. ____

10. If the cosmetologist uses too much pressure on Carl's hair, it may cause:

   A. skin discoloration.
   B. hair breakage.
   C. the hair to become lubricated.
   D. curl reversion. ____

11. What should the cosmetologist do for Isianita's scalp burn?

   A. apply an antiseptic salve
   B. apply a disinfectant solution
   C. spray it with water
   D. apply a hot compress ____

12. What type of press did Carl receive? A __________ press.

   A. cool
   B. hard
   C. medium
   D. soft ____

---

13. It is early in the morning and you notice on the appointment book that at 3:00 P.M. you have a client who has scheduled a "silking" service. This is the same as a:

   A. deep conditioner/reconstructor.
   B. chemical hair relaxer.
   C. shampoo and blow-dry.
   D. thermal press. ____

14. At 3:00 P.M., the "silking" client comes into your salon. The hair is medium texture, 5 inches long, and chemically relaxed. You:

   A. proceed with the scheduled service.
   B. inform the client that hair of her texture cannot be silked.
   C. inform her that relaxed hair cannot be silked.
   D. cut 3 inches of hair off before silking it. ____

SITUATION FOR ITEMS 15–18:

The owner of the salon has decided to buy new thermal straightening combs. What is wanted is the best quality implements for the best price. To find them, the salon owner will shop around before making the final choice. A decision has to be made between regular pressing combs and electric ones.

15. Thermal combs are made of:
    1. high-grade steel
    2. brass
    3. hard rubber
    4. plastic

    A. 1 and 2
    B. 2 and 3
    C. 1 and 4
    D. 1 only ___

16. A regular pressing comb is heated by:

    A. immersion in hot water.
    B. an oven/stove.
    C. attaching it to the nozzle of a blow dryer.
    D. a thermostat on the comb. ___

17. The handle of a pressing comb is made of:

    A. high-grade steel.
    B. brass.
    C. wood.
    D. plastic. ___

18. An electric pressing comb is heated by:

    A. immersion in hot water.
    B. an oven/stove.
    C. attaching it to the nozzle of a blow dryer.
    D. a thermostat on the comb. ___

---

19. Ruby has fine hair; Lolita has wiry, curly hair; Perry has medium hair; and Eddie has coarse hair. Whose hair will require the most heat and pressure when getting pressed?

    A. Ruby
    B. Lolita
    C. Perry
    D. Eddie ___

20. It has been a very hot and humid week. A client that you thermally straightened just a few days ago has come to you today because some of her hair has become curly again with all of the humidity. You press the hair without shampooing it. This is called a:

A. touch-up.
B. redo.
C. chemical relaxer.
D. dehumidifying treatment. ____

15. The Artistry of Artificial Hair

1. To increase income, Keiko has decided to include artificial hair, or wiggery, in her salon. Which of the following are included in a salon's use of wigs? Wig:
   1. sales
   2. sanitation
   3. styling
   4. servicing

   A. 1 and 2
   B. 1, 3, and 4
   C. 2 and 3
   D. 1, 2, 3, and 4 ____

2. Your client has brought an old wig into the salon. The client does not know if it is made of human hair or synthetic hair. In order to determine what it is made of, you perform a ____________ test.

   A. patch
   B. strand
   C. fingernail
   D. match ____

3. The wig you are styling is a very inexpensive one. This means that it is:

   A. hand knotted.
   B. machine sewn.
   C. made of human hair.
   D. on a fine mesh foundation. ____

4. Carmela has artificial hair braided, or interwoven, onto her existing hair to give her added thickness and length. What Carmela has is called:

   A. a toupee.
   B. a wiglet.
   C. extensions.
   D. cascades. ____

SITUATION FOR ITEMS 5–6:

To compensate for his bald spot, Alberto wears a hairpiece all of the time. He has been wearing one for 5 years and wouldn't be seen without it.

5. Alberto's type of hairpiece is called a/an:
   A. toupee.
   B. wiglet.
   C. extension.
   D. cascade. ___

6. How does Alberto's hairpiece stay on his scalp?
   A. T-pins
   B. clippies
   C. adhesive
   D. it is sewn onto braids ___

7. You are measuring your client's head for a wig. All of the following measurements are to be taken **EXCEPT**:
   A. the neck's circumference.
   B. the head's circumference.
   C. from ear to ear across the forehead.
   D. from ear to ear over the top of the head. ___

8. Kim, your client, really loves the wig she is trying on. It is just the right color and length for her. Unfortunately, it fits too tightly on her head. In order for it to fit Kim, you wet it and then:
   A. let it dry naturally on a smaller block.
   B. blow it dry on Kim's head.
   C. dry it with heat on a larger block.
   D. let it dry naturally on a larger block. ___

9. How should Karam clean his human hair wig? By:
   A. using laundry detergent.
   B. dry-cleaning fluid.
   C. using powder-dry shampoo.
   D. washing it in hot, soapy water. ___

SITUATION FOR ITEMS 10–12:

Hanh has brought you a brand new wig she just bought on sale. She would like you to cut it so that it looks better on her than it does now. Hanh does not know if the wig is a synthetic or human hair wig. Before anything else, you perform the test to determine its type of hair.

10. Your test results tell you that Hanh's wig is made of synthetic hair. If it had been made out of human hair, during the test the hair would have:

    A. had little, or no smell/odor.
    B. burned quickly.
    C. balled up on the ends.
    D. had a strong smell/odor. ___

11. Hanh's synthetic wig should be cut:

    A. dry.
    B. wet.
    C. damp.
    D. either wet or dry. ___

12. Synthetic wigs can be cut in length with a:

    A. razor.
    B. scissor/shear.
    C. nipper.
    D. thinning shear. ___

SITUATION FOR ITEMS 13–15:

Manuel's client has left her wig at his salon for Manuel to set/style. She will return in a week to pick it up. After cleaning it, Manuel notices that the hair on the wig is dry and brittle. His client told him that she wants it styled close to the face in front so that it won't appear like a wig.

13. What should Manuel do to get rid of the dryness/brittleness?

    A. clean it again
    B. use fabric softener
    C. condition it
    D. lubricate it ___

14. In order to set it, Manuel will need to place the wig on:

   A. a mannequin with hair.
   B. another person's head.
   C. a block.
   D. a styling station. ___

15. To achieve the desired style, Manuel should set the hair at the front hairline using __________ curls.

   A. pin
   B. cascade
   C. stand-up
   D. barrel ___

---

16. Your client has a human hair wig and would like you to darken the color of it. Which of the following may be safely used on human hairpieces?
   1. temporary rinses
   2. semi-permanent hair color
   3. permanent hair color
   4. lightener/bleach

   A. 1 and 2
   B. 1, 3, and 4
   C. 2 and 3
   D. 3 and 4 ___

17. Molly has a hairpiece that has a colored headband sewn into it. She can change the headband to match her clothes. This type of hairpiece is a:

   A. switch.
   B. wiglet.
   C. fall.
   D. bandeau. ___

18. Van is measuring Chana's head for a wig. What does Van use to measure the head? A:

   A. ruler.
   B. tape measure.
   C. hydrometer.
   D. yardstick. ___

19. You are styling a client's wig. It is securely fastened to a block that is:

A. absorbent.
B. smaller than the client's head.
C. made of canvas.
D. porous. ___

20. Jose is ordering a wiglet by mail for his client. He wants it to match the natural hair color perfectly. What should he do?

A. verbally inform the manufacturer of the color
B. send a bottle of similar permanent hair color with the order
C. send a sample of another wig with the order
D. send samples of the client's hair with the order ___

16. Manicuring and Pedicuring

1. You are just beginning to do a manicure on a client and notice tinea on her hands. You are to:

   A. refuse the service.
   B. continue with the service.
   C. soak the hands in soapy water.
   D. have the client wipe her hands in ammonia. ____

2. Your client Jean has artificial nails on her fingers. What type of nail polish remover are you to use?

   A. alcohol
   B. nonalcohol
   C. acetone
   D. non-acetone ____

3. You apply cuticle cream to Mark's cuticles while giving him a manicure. What does this cream do to the cuticles?

   A. bleaches them
   B. softens them
   C. hardens them
   D. adheres them ____

4. Client's fingernails are to be filed:

   A. center to corner.
   B. corner to center.
   C. back and forth.
   D. from one corner to the other in one stroke. ____

5. You are applying artificial nails using a nail form. What kind of artificial nails are you applying?

   A. press-on nails
   B. nail tips
   C. sculptured nails
   D. acrylic over nail tips ____

SITUATION FOR ITEMS 6–9:

Joe, a construction worker, is here for his very first manicure.

6. His cuticles and nails are very dry and cracked. What type of manicure should you give him?

   A. basic
   B. cold oil
   C. hot oil
   D. booth
   ___

7. Which implement do you use to push back and loosen his cuticles?

   A. cuticle nippers
   B. nail brush
   C. cushion
   D. orangewood stick
   ___

8. Which implement do you use to shape the free edges of his nails?

   A. emery board
   B. nail buffer
   C. orangewood stick
   D. cuticle scissors
   ___

9. How often do you suggest that Joe receive a regular manicure?

   A. once a year
   B. once a month
   C. once a week
   D. once a day
   ___

SITUATION FOR ITEMS 10–11:

Monica's nails are stained from her own applications of bright red nail polish.

10. Why did Monica's nails get so stained? Because of:

    A. not using top coat over the red polish.
    B. improper nail filing.
    C. not using a base coat over the nail.
    D. Monica's application of a coat of red polish on top of the old polish every day.
    ___

11. What nail cosmetic can you use to remove these stains from her nails?

    A. cuticle solvent
    B. nail bleach
    C. nail polish thinner
    D. alum ___

---

12. What can be applied underneath the free edges of Helena's nails to make them appear white?

    A. alum
    B. nail bleach
    C. nail cleanser
    D. nail whiteners ___

13. To prevent Barbara's nail polish from chipping, you should apply a/an:

    A. extra coat of polish.
    B. base coat.
    C. spray nail dry.
    D. top coat. ___

14. Anthony's nails peel and split easily. To prevent this, you should suggest that he:

    A. use nail hardener/strengthener.
    B. use base coat.
    C. buff his nails.
    D. use alum. ___

15. When giving a manicure, metal implements (such as your cuticle nippers) are to be kept on the manicuring table in a:

    A. closed drawer.
    B. sterilizer jar.
    C. small implement box.
    D. neat row on top of a clean towel. ___

16. In this container (item number 15 above), there should also be:

    A. 3% hydrogen peroxide.
    B. 6% hydrogen peroxide.
    C. 7% alcohol.
    D. 70% alcohol. ___

17. What does the nail technician use to remove a semisolid cream from its container/jar?

A. a shaker
B. her fingers
C. a spatula
D. nail wrap

___

18. Jerome is performing a pedicure on a client. How should he shape the toenails? Into a/an ______________ shape.

A. pointed
B. oval
C. round
D. straight-across

___

19. While cutting excessive cuticle around the nail, Jessica accidentally cuts the client's skin so that it bleeds. What should Jessica use to stop this bleeding?

A. alum
B. alcohol
C. acetone
D. non-acetone

___

20. Which of the following can Brian use to sanitize his manicuring implements? A/an:

A. disinfectant.
B. antiseptic.
C. formaldehyde-based nail hardener.
D. acetone remover.

___

21. Mary has two nails that are split but she does not want to shorten her nails. In order to keep them long, which of the following can she use to repair her two split nails?

A. nail conditioner
B. mending tissue
C. alum
D. collagen protein

___

22. Richard is just beginning a basic manicure. What is the proper procedural order that he is to follow?
    1. shape nails
    2. polish the nails
    3. remove old polish
    4. loosen cuticle; clean under free edge
    5. soak in finger bowl

    A. 3, 5, 2, 4, 1
    B. 3, 1, 5, 4, 2
    C. 1, 3, 4, 2, 5
    D. 5, 3, 1, 4, 2 ____

23. How can Carly remove nail polish that accidentally got on the client's skin? By using:

    A. an orangewood stick with cotton and polish remover.
    B. an orangewood stick with cotton and cuticle remover.
    C. a cotton swab with nail cleanser.
    D. a cotton ball with polish thinner. ____

24. Gabriel is a nail technician. He shapes most of his client's fingernails into the ideal nail shape, which is considered to be the ______________ shape.

    A. square
    B. round (or clubbed)
    C. oval
    D. slender tapered (or pointed) ____

25. How often should a nail technician include a hand massage when performing manicures?

    A. as part of each manicure
    B. in hot oil manicures only
    C. only for clients with dry skin
    D. only for clients who have artificial nails applied ____

26. Rebecca's Nail Salon offers manicures that use a portable device with a small motor. What type of manicure is this?

    A. oil
    B. booth
    C. electric
    D. retouch ____

27. Sandy's Styling Salon offers manicures to their clients while they are receiving other services. They are not performed at a manicuring table. This is called a/an __________ manicure.

A. oil
B. booth
C. electric
D. machine ____

28. Kim is explaining to her client the advantages of artificial nails. In her discussion, she can include all of the following **EXCEPT**:

A. they conceal damaged nails.
B. they can help stop nail biting.
C. they protect against nail splitting.
D. they prevent the spread of nail disease. ____

29. Maria is applying nail wraps to her client's nails. Before adhering the mending tissue to the nails, Maria:

A. applies base coat to the nail.
B. applies adhesive underneath the free edge.
C. trims the tissue to fit the nail.
D. adheres a nail tip to the nail plate. ____

30. In order to apply sculptured nails on his client, which of the following product supplies will Terrence need?

1. acrylic powder
2. nail adhesive
3. acrylic liquid
4. nail forms
5. acetone liquid

A. 1, 2, and 5
B. 1, 3, and 4
C. 2, 3, and 5
D. 3, 4, and 5 ____

31. Terry has noticed that many nail hardeners contain the same ingredient. That ingredient is:

A. ammonia.
B. sodium hydroxide.
C. sodium bromate.
D. formaldehyde. ____

32. What is the correct procedure for Ashley to apply acrylic nails on a client?

A. dip the brush into the liquid, then twirl it in the powder
B. apply liquid to the nail plate, then dip the nail into a dish of powder
C. dip the brush into the powder, then dip it into the liquid
D. dip the client's nail into the powder, then brush on the liquid ___

33. Before applying artificial nails, how should Tom prepare the client's natural nails?

A. soak them in warm, soapy water
B. apply nail hardener to them
C. soak them in hot oil
D. gently roughen them with a file ___

SITUATION FOR ITEMS 34–36:

Trinette had sculptured nails applied to her nails 6 weeks ago. They have grown out and lifted from her nail plate. She has not gone back to the salon for fills or repairs, and now her natural nail has changed its color.

34. This change in color is due to:

A. her base coat has stained her nail.
B. a fungus that has begun to grow.
C. her nail has absorbed her colorless dishwashing liquid.
D. the fact that all acrylic changes color after 6 weeks. ___

35. This condition is to be treated by:

A. Trinette.
B. a nail technician.
C. a physician.
D. an instructor. ___

36. It could help to avoid this type of situation if the nail technician does **NOT** touch the client's nail after the:

A. primer is applied.
B. acrylic is applied.
C. acrylic is filed.
D. polish is applied. ___

---

37. The press-on nails (also referred to as nail tips) Sue applied to Tracy's fingers are made out of:

A. plastic (or nylon).
B. liquid and powder.
C. adhesive/glue and powder.
D. gel or wax. ___

38. What type of nail polish remover should Sue use on Tracy's nail tips when changing the color of polish?

A. acetone
B. non-acetone
C. acetate
D. alcohol ___

39. The nail technician must be careful with smoking, matches, and lighters because a particular nail product is very flammable. This product is a nail:

A. polish.
B. form.
C. adhesive/glue.
D. brush. ___

40. Shelly has nail tips on her fingernails that she wants removed. To do this, fill a small container and soak the nail tips in:

A. a non-acetone polish remover.
B. a mixture of alum and water.
C. an adhesive solvent.
D. 70% alcohol. ___

41. While giving a pedicure, you notice that your client has corns, calluses, and ingrown nails. These conditions should be treated by a:

A. cosmetologist.
B. salon manager.
C. nail technician.
D. podiatrist. ___

SITUATION FOR ITEMS 42–43:

Your client, Andrew, has athlete's foot.

42. The technical name for this condition is:

A. pityriasis.
B. pediculosis.
C. alopecia.
D. tinea. ___

43. Athlete's foot is considered to be:

A. contagious.
B. noncontagious.
C. hereditary.
D. acute. ___

---

44. Before removing the old polish on Wendy's toenails, the feet, and/or toenails, should first:

A. be massaged with foot oil.
B. be soaked in an antiseptic foot bath.
C. filed straight across.
D. have their excessive cuticles cut off. ___

45. To avoid ingrown nails when performing a pedicure on Conrad:

A. file the nails into a pointed shape.
B. file into the corners of the nails.
C. do not file into the corners of the nails.
D. do not file the nails at all. ___

46. You are performing a pedicure on Shirley. The foot massage is to be performed:

A. after the soaking and filing and before applying polish.
B. after applying polish and before the soaking.
C. after the soaking and before filing the nails and loosening the cuticles.
D. after the soaking and before removing the old polish. ___

47. Your pedicure client has very callused, dry, and cracked skin on their feet. What would you include in your pedicure in this situation?

A. remove the calluses with your cuticle nippers
B. file the calluses down with your emery board
C. use hot oil and perform a thorough foot massage
D. soak the feet in 70% alcohol ___

48. An adhesive (glue) is used when performing the following artificial nail services:

1. nail tips
2. acrylic nails (only)
3. press-on nails

A. 1 only
B. 1 and 3
C. 2 and 3
D. 1, 2, and 3 ___

49. Ava wants some nail ornaments (jewels and stripes) applied to her nails. When do you apply these?

   A. after applying the base coat
   B. after filing the nails
   C. after the hand and arm massage
   D. after applying the polish ___

50. Applying polish to the toenails can be difficult because the toes are so close together. What is the nail technician to use in order to separate the toes?

   A. the fingers
   B. cotton
   C. a towel
   D. orangewood sticks ___

17. The Nail and Its Disorders

SITUATION FOR ITEMS 1–3:

Brenda is a very curious client. While getting a manicure, she asks the nail technician many questions about nails.

1. You inform her that nails, just like hair, are appendages of the:

   A. fingers.
   B. toes.
   C. skin.
   D. matrix. ___

2. She asks you what is the technical term for the nails. Your reply is:

   A. tricho.
   B. onyx.
   C. matrix.
   D. nail bed. ___

3. Brenda does not have a half-moon on all of her fingernails. You inform her that another term for this part of the nail is the:

   A. lunula.
   B. lanugo.
   C. free edge.
   D. hyponychium. ___

SITUATION FOR ITEMS 4–8:

Owen was in an accident and three of his nails were ripped ¼ inch below his free edge.

4. Owen's fingers hurt a lot because the skin under the nail contains many:

   A. bones.
   B. melanin.
   C. suderiferous glands.
   D. nerve endings. ___

5. The skin on which the nail rests is called the nail:

   A. body.
   B. bed.
   C. wall.
   D. groove. ___

6. Owen wants to know how fast his nails will grow back. You inform him that the average monthly rate of growth of nails is about _________ of an inch.

   A. 1⁄16
   B. ⅛
   C. ¼
   D. ½ ___

7. Under which condition will Owen's nails grow back and be healthy?

   A. if there is no damage to the matrix
   B. if the matrix is severely damaged
   C. if the nail and its surrounding tissue get infected
   D. if the nail bed sustains damage ___

8. If Owen's entire nail had been removed in the accident, approximately how long would it take for a new nail to grow?

   A. 1 week
   B. 2 months
   C. 4 months
   D. 1 year ___

---

9. Filing the nails is not painful for the client, because:

   A. the nails are made of keratin.
   B. the nails are farthest from the heart.
   C. blood vessels are not found near the matrix.
   D. the nail plate does not contain nerve endings. ___

SITUATION FOR ITEMS 10–13:

A well-known nail technician is giving a class on the nails and new nail products. The first 20 minutes of the class is a review of the nail and its structures. You are a participant of this class.

10. The nail technician asks, "Of what substance are nails made?" Your reply is:

    A. keratin
    B. melanin
    C. sodium
    D. lymph ___

11. The next question asked is: "Is the nail plate one piece?" Your response is:

    A. yes, it is one solid piece.
    B. yes, but it is constructed in layers.
    C. no, it is many little pieces glued together.
    D. no, it is made of horizontal strips stuck together. ___

12. "What is the name of the tracks on the sides of the nail along which it moves?" is the third question asked by the nail technician. Your response is:

    A. nail walls.
    B. mantle.
    C. nail grooves.
    D. hyponychium. ___

13. The final question of this review is: "What is the name of the portion of the epidermis that is under the free edge of the nail?"

    A. mantle
    B. eponychium
    C. perionychium
    D. hyponychium ___

---

14. Of the people listed below, whose nails grow faster?

    Ed, a 76-year-old man
    Victoria, Ed's 56-year-old daughter
    Greg, Victoria's 2-year-old grandson

    A. Ed's
    B. Victoria's
    C. Greg's
    D. All nails grow at the same rate. ___

15. Sarah, a nail technician, can perform nail services on the following:

A. an inflamed cuticle.
B. athlete's foot.
C. an infected nail bed.
D. simple nail irregularities. ____

16. Theo has white spots on his nails. The technical term for these spots is:

A. leuconychia.
B. corrugations.
C. onychauxis.
D. onychatrophia. ____

17. Elissa's nail plate became smaller until it finally shed off. What is the name of this irregularity?

A. onychatrophia
B. onychorrhexis
C. blue nails
D. agnail ____

18. Ron bites his nails. The technical term for this is:

A. onychorrhexis.
B. pterygium.
C. onychophagy.
D. furrows. ____

19. Your best friend's grandmother, Florence, is receiving a manicure from you today. You notice that she has blue nails. This may be a sign of:

A. a nervous disorder.
B. poor blood circulation.
C. a contagious nail disease.
D. her skin's melanin color. ____

SITUATION FOR ITEMS 20–21:

Dawn's physician has diagnosed that she has tinea of the nails.

20. Which of the following is another term for this disease?

A. ringworm
B. white spots
C. lice
D. ingrown nails ____

21. Which of the following is characteristic of Dawn's disease? It is:

A. not contagious.
B. contagious.
C. an animal parasite.
D. caused by a nervous disorder. ___

SITUATION FOR ITEMS 22–23:

Trevor has two ingrown toenails.

22. The technical term for this is:

A. onychoptosis.
B. onychogryposis.
C. tinea unguium.
D. onychocrypotosis. ___

23. This probably happened to Trevor because of:

1. improper filing of the nails
2. not wearing stockings with his shoes
3. ill-fitting shoes
4. improper sitting posture

A. 1 and 4
B. 1 and 3
C. 1, 3, and 4
D. 2, 3, and 4 ___

---

24. The wavy ridges on Marion's nails are called:

A. corrugations.
B. leuconychia.
C. onychatrophia.
D. onychauxis. ___

25. Your client wants to know where her nail begins to grow. The answer to this is the nail:

A. eponychium.
B. cuticle.
C. matrix.
D. hyponychium. ___

26. While performing a pedicure on a client, you notice that his feet are full of watery blisters. You:

    A. continue with the service.
    B. pop/break the blisters.
    C. refuse to work on the feet until the condition heals.
    D. after the massage, wrap the feet in hot towels saturated with an antiseptic. ____

SITUATION FOR ITEMS 27–29:

Osmond's nails are in very bad condition. The overlapping skin around the nail is excessive and very dry. In some areas, this skin has split.

27. The name of this overlapping skin is the:

    A. hyponychium.
    B. lunula.
    C. free edge.
    D. cuticle. ____

28. The areas that are split are called:

    A. mantles.
    B. hangnails.
    C. bruised nails.
    D. blue nails. ____

29. What type of manicure should Osmond receieve? A __________ manicure.

    A. booth
    B. basic
    C. hot oil
    D. mini ____

---

30. Your client wants her nails shorter. What is the name of the part of the nail that you file in order to shorten the nails?

    A. nail bed
    B. lunula
    C. eponychium
    D. free edge ____

31. When examining the hands, fingers, and nails immediately before giving a manicure, you want to make sure that the color of healthy nails appears slightly:

    A. pink.
    B. blue.
    C. red.
    D. yellow. ___

SITUATION FOR ITEMS 32–33:

Avis's nails got smashed in a window and have dark, purplish spots on them.

32. The name for Avis's condition is:

    A. blue nails.
    B. bruised nails.
    C. onychorrhexis.
    D. onychophagy. ___

33. These dark spots are actually:

    A. damaged nerve endings.
    B. dried blood.
    C. old nail polish.
    D. abnormal keratin deposits. ___

18. Theory of Massage

1. While massaging your client's shoulders, you use a kneading movement. This is called:

   A. effleurage
   B. petrissage.
   C. tapotement.
   D. friction. ___

2. Chucking, rolling, and wringing are movements that Melanie uses when she massages her client's arm. Chucking, rolling, and wringing are three forms of:

   A. effleurage.
   B. petrissage.
   C. vibration.
   D. friction. ___

3. Lynn receives a weekly facial massage. What does the massage do for her blood circulation? It:

   A. increases.
   B. weakens.
   C. decreases.
   D. soothes. ___

4. Wayne is performing the vibration massage movement on his client. Another name for this is:

   A. chucking
   B. kneading.
   C. shaking.
   D. rolling. ___

5. Louise's arms are receiving a type of petrissage movement. This light pressure movement under Louise's forearm is also known as:

   A. fulling.
   B. wringing.
   C. slapping.
   D. hacking. ____

SITUATION FOR ITEMS 6–7:

Tyler is receiving the most stimulating massage movement on his shoulders and back. His cosmetologist's wrists and fingers are touching his skin in rapid succession.

6. What massage movement is Tyler receiving?

   A. vibration
   B. tapotement
   C. friction
   D. petrissage ____

7. This massage manipulation Tyler is receiving includes:
   1. tapping
   2. slapping
   3. rolling
   4. hacking
   5. kneading

   A. 1 and 2
   B. 1, 2, and 3
   C. 1, 2, and 4
   D. 2, 4, and 5 ____

---

8. Your client is hesitant to receive a facial massage. During your consultation, you try to list all of the benefits of facial massage that you can remember. This includes all of the following **EXCEPT**:

   A. strengthens/tones muscles.
   B. makes skin soft and pliable.
   C. soothes facial nerves.
   D. decreases blood circulation. ____

9. Laura is applying light, continuous stroking movements to her client's face. This is called:

   A. effleurage.
   B. petrissage.
   C. vibration.
   D. tapotement. ____

10. Lois is performing a facial massage on Bob. The direction of her manipulations is important to prevent Bob's skin from sagging. Her massage movements are to be from:

    A. origin of a muscle toward its insertion.
    B. forehead toward neck.
    C. insertion of a muscle toward its origin.
    D. outside of face toward the mouth. ___

19. Facials

1. Toni is receiving a facial to help her skin condition. She has blackheads. What type of facial is she receiving?

   A. preservative
   B. corrective
   C. maintenance
   D. wax ___

2. Eduardo is performing a facial on his client. He removes the semisolid creams from their containers by using:

   A. his clean fingers.
   B. his soiled fingers.
   C. a soiled spatula.
   D. a sanitary spatula. ___

3. While receiving a facial, the following parts of Marion are to be draped/covered:

   1. hands
   2. neck
   3. chest
   4. hair

   A. 1 only
   B. 1 and 2
   C. 2 and 3
   D. 3 and 4 ___

4. During a facial, when is the massage performed?

   A. after the cleansing cream is removed
   B. after the toner/astringent is applied
   C. before the cleansing cream is applied
   D. after the moisturizer is applied ___

SITUATION FOR ITEMS 5–6:

In the services offered at The Terrace Hair Salon, use of an infrared lamp is included in the facial service for clients.

5. Infrared rays produce:
   A. tanning/darkening of the skin.
   B. disinfecting vapors.
   C. heat.
   D. moisture. ___

6. Whenever you use infrared rays on the face:
   A. leave an ample amount of emulsion on the skin.
   B. the lamp should be 5 inches from the face.
   C. a minimum of 20 minutes is essential.
   D. protect the eyes with pads. ___

---

7. Your client's facial cheeks have whiteheads. The technical name for this is:
   A. miliara rubra.
   B. comedone.
   C. milia.
   D. sebum. ___

8. Chao is using a galvanic current with a positive charge on his client. This charge causes:
   A. the pores to open.
   B. the pores to close.
   C. a decrease in the suderiferous glands.
   D. the skin to weaken. ___

SITUATION FOR ITEMS 9–12:

Ruth has extremely dry skin and would like a series of facial treatments to help improve this condition. She has come to you today for her first facial treatment. The facial toners/astringents for use in your salon include:

Brand W = contains no alcohol
Brand X = contains 35% alcohol
Brand Y = contains 50% alcohol
Brand Z = contains 70% alcohol

9. The name of the natural oil that Ruth's skin lacks is:
   A. keratin.
   B. sebum.
   C. suderiferous.
   D. melanin. ___

10. The gland that secretes this oil is the __________ gland.
    A. sebaceous
    B. apocrine
    C. eccrine
    D. suderiferous ___

11. The most beneficial facial that you could give Ruth would include:
    1. a facial pack
    2. a facial mask
    3. an astringent with alcohol
    4. electrical current

    A. 1 and 3
    B. 2 and 3
    C. 2 and 4
    D. 3 and 4 ___

12. Which toner/astringent should you use on Ruth?
    A. Brand W
    B. Brand X
    C. Brand Y
    D. Brand Z ___

13. When performing a facial, when does Tammy analyze her client's skin?

    A. after the massage
    B. immediately before applying the astringent
    C. before removing the client's make-up
    D. after the cleansing cream is removed ___

14. Juanita has been applying negative galvanic current to Ninh's face for the past 4 minutes. What is this doing to Ninh's face?

    A. cleansing it
    B. decreasing the activity of his suderiferous glands
    C. opening his pores
    D. closing his pores ___

15. Jerry is applying a customized facial mask using fresh fruit. To help this stay on the skin, he must use a mask made out of:

    A. hot oil.
    B. gauze.
    C. wax.
    D. tissue paper. ___

SITUATION FOR ITEMS 16–18:

Beth is your facial client who has just arrived for her appointment. She is wearing a lot of makeup, so it is difficult to see her skin very well. The earrings and necklace she is wearing are very large. You escort her to the facial area, which is 30 feet from your station and the shampoo bowls. After draping, consulting, and cleansing her skin, you discover that she has very oily skin.

16. Where should Beth's jewelry be stored during her facial?

    A. in her purse or clothing pockets
    B. at your hairstyling station
    C. in the shampoo bowl area of the salon
    D. in the reception area ___

17. Which of the following should be included in your facial on Beth? A/an:

    1. facial pack
    2. facial mask
    3. astringent with alcohol
    4. toner without alcohol

    A. 1 only
    B. 1 and 3
    C. 2 and 3
    D. 2 and 4 ___

18. Your analysis of Beth's skin made you realize that she has oily skin. All of the following are also determined by the skin's analysis **EXCEPT**:

    A. the choice of products to be used on her.
    B. the skin's natural color and texture.
    C. areas that need special attention.
    D. the amounts and colors of makeup she uses. ___

SITUATION FOR ITEMS 19–21:

You have four facial appointments for today. Your analysis of their skin types is as follows: Mario has acne; Marguerite has blackheads; Yen-Seng's skin is very dry; and Paula has extremely oily skin.

19. Which client do you refer to a physician?

    A. Mario
    B. Marguerite
    C. Yen-Seng
    D. Paula ___

20. Marguerite's condition is also known as:

    A. milia.
    B. acne.
    C. comedone.
    D. furuncle. ___

21. On which client do you use a toner/astringent that contains little or no alcohol?

    A. Mario
    B. Marguerite
    C. Yen-Seng
    D. Paula ___

---

22. Gen has healthy, glowing skin. She wants a facial because it relaxes her. What type of facial do you perform on Gen?

    A. preservative
    B. highly stimulating
    C. corrective
    D. invigorating ___

23. The cream you have just applied to your client's face immediately itches, burns, and/or irritates her skin. You:

A. spray water on top of the cream to dilute it.
B. remove the cream immediately.
C. apply an antiseptic over the cream.
D. continue with the facial. ___

24. While draping your client's hair for a facial, you notice that he has pediculosis. You:

A. give him a facial without a massage.
B. give him a facial with galvanic current.
C. continue with the service.
D. refuse to continue with the service. ___

25. Liv is in your salon for her first professional facial treatment. During your consultation, you discuss many benefits of facials. These include all of the following **EXCEPT**:

A. activating glandular activity.
B. decreasing blood circulation.
C. strengthening weak muscles.
D. softening skin texture. ___

20. Facial Makeup

SITUATION FOR ITEMS 1–6:

Caroline and Alice have makeup appointments with you. Caroline has a broad jaw, and close-set eyes with dark circles under them. Alice has wide-set eyes, a short, thick neck, and a broad nose.

1. To diminish the dark circles under Caroline's eyes, you:

   A. shadow the circle areas.
   B. apply a darker foundation over the circles.
   C. use a rose-color blush.
   D. apply a lighter foundation over the circles. ____

2. To make Alice's eyes appear closer together, you:

   A. extend the eyebrow line toward the inside corners of her eyes.
   B. extend the outside of the eyebrow line.
   C. increase the arch of the eyebrow.
   D. give the eyebrow a straight-across shape. ____

3. What do you do to make Alice's neck appear thinner?

   A. use lighter foundation on it
   B. use darker foundation on it
   C. use highlighter on it
   D. use darker foundation on the face ____

4. To help Caroline's eyes appear farther apart, you:

   A. apply shadow up from the eye's outer edge.
   B. apply shadow inward toward the nose.
   C. highlight under the eyes.
   D. highlight under the eyebrow's highest point. ____

5. To diminish Caroline's jaw, you:

   A. apply lighter foundation in the jaw area.
   B. use translucent powder along the jawline.
   C. apply darker foundation in the jaw area.
   D. highlight the entire jaw area. ___

6. What do you do to make Alice's nose appear thinner?

   A. use light foundation on the sides of the nose
   B. apply dark foundation down the center of the nose
   C. use dark foundation on the sides of the nose
   D. apply dark foundation under the nose ___

---

7. Thai is tinting his client's eyelashes and brows. He is careful with using the proper product near his client's eyes. Aniline derivative tints should never be used on lashes or brows because they may cause:

   A. herpes simplex.
   B. blindness.
   C. canities.
   D. monilethrix. ___

8. As Natalie arches her client's eyebrows, she is to pull the hair quickly and:

   A. against its natural growth direction.
   B. in the same direction as its natural growth.
   C. out from the skin.
   D. toward the client's forehead, or upward. ___

SITUATION FOR ITEMS 9–11:

Felix is applying individual, artificial eyelashes to his client's own eyelashes.

9. This is called:

   A. feather-lashing.
   B. strip eyelashes.
   C. lash retouching.
   D. eye tabbing. ___

10. How many weeks do these eyelashes stay on the client's eyelashes?

    A. 1
    B. 2
    C. 4
    D. 6–8 ___

11. The length of lashes that Felix uses on his client's lower lashes should be:

   A. short.
   B. medium.
   C. long.
   D. 1 inch. ___

---

12. Doreen creates a line on her eyelid close to her lashes in order for her eyes to appear larger and her lashes fuller. She does this by using:

   A. eye shadow.
   B. eyebrow pencil.
   C. eyeliner.
   D. mascara. ___

13. Your client has an oval facial shape which means that the distance between her eyes is:

   A. 1 inch.
   B. the width of her lips.
   C. the length of her nose.
   D. the width of one eye. ___

SITUATION FOR ITEMS 14–15:

You are arching your client's eyebrows and notice that the natural arch of her eyebrow follows the curve of her eye socket. As you proceed with the arch, you pull tautly on the skin and wipe the brow with cotton.

14. Another name for the eye socket's curve is the:

   A. orbit.
   B. capilli.
   C. lunula.
   D. flagella. ___

15. The cotton you use should be moistened with:

   A. a disinfectant.
   B. 20-volume hydrogen peroxide.
   C. an antiseptic.
   D. 70% alcohol. ___

SITUATION FOR ITEMS 16–21:

Hoang is a makeup artist. He is preparing four clients for a fashion show. Andrea has a square-shaped face. Helena's face is pear-shaped. Jane has a diamond-shaped face with close-set eyes. Sue's face is oblong, or long.

16. To make Jane's eyes appear farther apart, Hoang is to:

    A. make the eyebrow arch very high.
    B. widen the distance between the eyebrows.
    C. make the eyebrows almost straight.
    D. shorten the distance between the eyebrows. ____

17. Sue's face can be given the illusion that it is shorter if Hoang:

    A. makes the eyebrow arch very high.
    B. widens the distance between the eyebrows.
    C. makes the eyebrows almost straight.
    D. shortens the distance between the eyebrows. ____

18. The person who has a narrow forehead and a wide jaw is:

    A. Andrea.
    B. Helena.
    C. Jane.
    D. Sue. ____

19. Andrea's makeup needs to:

    A. increase the width of her jaw.
    B. decrease her pointed chin.
    C. increase the width of her forehead.
    D. soften the hard lines around her face. ____

20. As Hoang applies makeup on Jane, he needs to:

    A. reduce her width at the cheekbones.
    B. reduce the width of her forehead.
    C. increase her width at the cheekbones.
    D. decrease her pointed chin. ____

21. Before applying makeup to his clients, Hoang:

    A. asks them to pay for the service.
    B. applies translucent powder to their skin.
    C. considers skin and eye colors, but not clothing.
    D. washes his hands. ____

22. Tim is applying a highlighter above his client's cheekbones. What does highlighter do?
    A. minimizes the feature
    B. gives a pink color
    C. emphasizes the feature
    D. darkens the area ___

23. Your client has applied her own makeup. Along her jaw, you can easily see where her foundation abruptly ends. This is a:
    A. blended application.
    B. line of demarcation.
    C. broad jawline.
    D. shadow line. ___

24. Before tinting a client's eyelashes, you are to:
    1. wash the lashes
    2. apply mascara
    3. apply cream and shields on the eyes
    4. apply strip lashes

    A. 1 and 3
    B. 1 and 4
    C. 2 and 3
    D. 1, 3, and 4 ___

25. Lucy is your client. She has an appointment for a makeup application, shampoo, and roller set. When do you apply the makeup?
    A. after the shampoo and before the roller set
    B. before the shampoo and roller set
    C. after the set and before the comb-out
    D. after the set and comb-out ___

21. The Skin and Its Disorders

SITUATION FOR ITEMS 1–3:

Your client plays tennis in the sun regularly. As a result, her skin is tan.

1. Which rays of the sun cause the skin to darken? ______________ rays.

   A. Infrared
   B. Ultraviolet
   C. Heat
   D. Light ___

2. The cells that produce skin color are called:

   A. basal.
   B. fat cells.
   C. papillae.
   D. melanocytes. ___

3. Skin color is made in the stratum:

   A. germinativum.
   B. granulosum.
   C. lucidum.
   D. corneum. ___

---

4. You accidentally touch your hot curling iron and quickly pull back your hand. The nerve fibers that responded to the heat are your ______________ nerve fibers.

   A. motor
   B. sensory
   C. secretory
   D. pressure ___

5. Hildur is a regular client of yours. She is 86 years old. Her skin is aged with a lot of wrinkles. This aging is due to her skin's loss of:

   A. dermis.
   B. melanin.
   C. elasticity.
   D. sebum. ___

6. The comedones on Randy's face are caused by hardened:

   A. melanin.
   B. keratin.
   C. sebum.
   D. perspiration. ___

SITUATION FOR ITEMS 7–10:

A client has entered the salon. Having just completed jogging 5 miles, the client is hot and sweaty.

7. The sweat glands are very active because they are performing their task of:

   A. heat regulation.
   B. secretion.
   C. protection.
   D. absorption. ___

8. If sweat is extremely foul-smelling, this client has:

   A. anhidrosis.
   B. miliaria rubra.
   C. hyperhidrosis.
   D. bromidrosis. ___

9. The reason sweat may have an offensive smell is that it:

   A. lubricates the skin.
   B. responds to heat.
   C. eliminates waste.
   D. protects from bacterial invasions. ___

10. Sweat glands are also known as ___________ glands.

    A. sebaceous
    B. suderiferous
    C. arrector pili
    D. subcutaneous ___

---

11. While performing a facial on Ginny, you notice that she has many facial macules. You are to:

    A. continue with the facial.
    B. apply an antiseptic to the macules before continuing.
    C. perform the facial, but eliminate the massage.
    D. refuse to continue with the facial. ___

12. Your client has informed you of her doctor's diagnosis of her disease. "Diagnosis" refers to a disease's:

    A. cause.
    B. future course.
    C. structure.
    D. recognition. ___

13. Loren was bitten by a mosquito 10 minutes ago. This bite is called a:

    A. bulla.
    B. cyst.
    C. tubercle.
    D. wheal. ___

SITUATION FOR ITEMS 14–18:

The following clients of yours have the following diseases: Drew has pediculosis; Anita cannot drink or eat milk products without having her body swell; Doug has AIDS; and Kwang has facial pimples.

14. What type of disease does Anita have?

    A. acute
    B. inflammatory
    C. allergy
    D. contagious ___

15. You could perform a haircut on all of these clients **EXCEPT**:

    A. Drew.
    B. Anita.
    C. Doug.
    D. Kwang. ___

16. Doug's disease is considered to be:

    A. acute.
    B. chronic.
    C. parasitic.
    D. vegetable-based. ___

17. Kwang's disease is characterized by a/an:

    A. objective lesion.
    B. excoriation.
    C. subjective lesion.
    D. stain. ___

18. Who has a parasitic disease?

    A. Drew
    B. Anita
    C. Doug
    D. Kwang ___

---

19. You are performing a hot oil manicure on Mr. Pham. His hands are so dry that his skin is cracked. These cracks are known as:

    A. ulcers.
    B. crusts.
    C. excoriations.
    D. fissures. ___

20. The client you are working on has excessively dry skin. This condition is called:

    A. seborrhea.
    B. rosacea.
    C. asteatosis.
    D. steatoma. ___

21. While giving a pedicure to Seiichi, you notice a keratoma. You are to:

    A. refuse to continue the pedicure.
    B. continue with the pedicure.
    C. refer Seiichi to a physician.
    D. use your orangewood stick to push the keratoma back. ___

22. Your client has asked you to remove the three hairs growing from a mole on her chin. You:

    A. remove the hairs.
    B. have her sign a release form, then remove the hairs.
    C. refuse to remove the hairs.
    D. soften the hairs with bleach, then gently pull them from their follicles. ___

23. The salon where you work has one employee who is licensed by the state to only perform skin care services. This person is licensed as a/an:

A. cosmetologist.
B. esthetician.
C. nail technician.
D. dermatologist. ___

24. Laurie is a client of yours who recently had plastic surgery on her nose. This procedure is called:

A. rhytidectomy.
B. dermabrasion.
C. blepharoplasty.
D. rhinoplasty. ___

SITUATION FOR ITEMS 25–29:

The cleansing cream has been removed from Jose's face. You are analyzing his skin closely with a magnifying glass. His skin feels smooth and looks like it is finely grained.

25. On which layer of Jose's skin was the cleansing cream? The:

A. epidermis's stratum corneum.
B. corium's stratum lucidum.
C. epidermis's stratum granulosum.
D. subcutaneous tissue. ___

26. Jose's skin is nourished by:

1. sweat
2. blood
3. keratin
4. oil
5. lymph

A. 1 and 2
B. 2 and 4
C. 2 and 5
D. 2, 3, and 4 ___

27. The words smooth and finely grained refer to Jose's skin's:

A. elasticity.
B. healthy color.
C. SP factor/SPF.
D. texture. ___

28. The skin is thinnest on Jose's:

A. cheeks.
B. eyelids.
C. forehead.
D. nose. ___

29. Which of the following is an appendage/s of Jose's skin? His:

A. nails.
B. arrector pili muscles.
C. papilla.
D. facial bones. ___

---

30. When cutting your client's hair, you accidentally cut your hand. The cut begins to bleed profusely. Before the cut could bleed, it had to reach which skin layer? The:

A. stratum lucidum.
B. epidermis.
C. dermis.
D. granular layer. ___

31. Scott is a 15-year-old with acne. He has made an appointment with you for a facial treatment. You:

A. use products with a high alcohol content.
B. suggest he see his physician.
C. perform a thorough facial massage on him.
D. perform the facial today, but suggest he see his physician if the facial does not clear the acne. ___

32. Myong has been diagnosed as having miliaria rubra. This is a disease of Myong's:

A. circulatory system.
B. oil glands.
C. melanocytes.
D. sweat glands. ___

33. Your client is an albino. This situation is:

A. acute.
B. communicable.
C. congenital.
D. acquired. ___

34. Your manicuring client is a writer by profession and has calluses on his fingers. These are caused by:

    A. continuous pressure.
    B. lack of attention.
    C. poor circulation.
    D. heredity. ___

SITUATION FOR ITEMS 35–39:

While performing a deep facial, you want to make sure that the second skin layer, or inner layer, is affected by the facial treatment.

35. The outermost skin layer is the:

    A. stratum mucosum.
    B. epidermis.
    C. subcutaneous tissue.
    D. dermis. ___

36. The underlying, or inner layer, is the:

    A. stratum lucidum.
    B. epidermis.
    C. hypodermis.
    D. dermis. ___

37. Which of the following is **NOT** found in the corium?

    A. blood vessels
    B. dead keratin cells
    C. nerves
    D. oil glands ___

38. The duct of the oil gland empties into the:

    A. epidermis.
    B. arrector pili muscle.
    C. suderiferous gland.
    D. hair follicle. ___

39. The two layers of the true skin are the:
    1. corneum
    2. granular
    3. papillary
    4. cuticle
    5. reticular

    A. 1 and 2
    B. 2 and 4
    C. 3 and 5
    D. 4 and 5 ___

SITUATION FOR ITEMS 40–41:

Dmitri's skin is excessively oily.

40. Which of Dmitri's glands controls this condition?

    A. sebaceous
    B. suderiferous
    C. apocrine
    D. eccrine ___

41. The name for the oil on Dmitri's skin is:

    A. melanin.
    D. keratin. ___
    C. milia.
    D. sebum. ___

42. In her excitement, goosebumps have appeared on Deborah's arms. What kind of nerve fibers have caused this?

    A. sensory
    B.motor
    C. pigment
    D. secretory ___

SITUATION FOR ITEMS 43–46:

Susan has fever blisters on her lips; Karen has a naevus on her ear; Lucian has warts on his hands; and Simon has lentigines on his face.

43. Another name for Susan's inflammation is:

    A. herpes simplex.
    B. eczema.
    C. psoriasis.
    D. chloasma. ___

44. Who has freckles?

    A. Simon
    B. Susan
    C. Lucian
    D. Karen ___

45. Karen's condition is commonly called a:

    A. liver spot.
    B. freckle.
    C. birthmark.
    D. white patch. ___

46. Lucian's warts are technically known as:

A. leucoderma.
B. vitiligo.
C. dermatitis venenata.
D. verruca.

___

47. The client you are working on has hyperhidrosis. This means that her perspiration is:

A. foul-smelling.
B. too little in its amount.
C. excessive.
D. normal.

___

48. Harry loves to eat and is overweight. In which layer of the skin are Harry's fat cells?

A. epidermis
B. dermis
C. subcutaneous tissue
D. corium

___

SITUATION FOR ITEMS 49–50:

Your client has poison ivy.

49. Her skin blisters are known as:

A. tubercles.
B. vesicles.
C. pustules.
D. cysts.

___

50. What type of lesion is this considered to be?

A. primary
B. secondary
C. tertiary
D. etiology

___

22. Removing Unwanted Hair

SITUATION FOR ITEMS 1–2:

Jenny would like to use a chemical product to remove the hair from her legs. She is nervous about this because her skin is sensitive and she has never done this before. A skin test is performed by placing the product on her arm.

1. The product she wants to use is called a/an:

   A. hot wax.
   B. epilator.
   C. depilatory.
   D. thermolysis. ___

2. The skin test burned her and turned her arm red. This means that Jenny can:

   A. use it on her legs.
   B. not use it on her skin at all.
   C. use it on her arms.
   D. not use it on her arms, but can use it on her legs. ___

---

3. Pam has a lot of unwanted hair on her face. She has sideburns and a moustache above her lips. This unwanted hair is called hypertrichosis, superfluous, and/or:

   A. capilli.
   B. vellus.
   C. canities.
   D. hirsutes. ___

4. After cutting Huai's hair, you clean his neck with your electric clippers. Using your clippers is a form of:

   A. depilation.
   B. electrolysis.
   C. shaving.
   D. electronic tweezing. ___

SITUATION FOR ITEMS 5–8:

Charlene is a licensed cosmetologist who also performs permanent hair removal on clients. She uses the thermolysis method of hair removal.

5. Besides being a cosmetologist, Charlene is also a/an:

   A. electrologist.
   B. esthetician.
   C. dermatologist.
   D. chemical technician. ___

6. Three areas from which Charlene should **NOT** remove hair are:

   1. lower eyelids
   2. chin
   3. inner ear
   4. nostrils
   5. upper lips
   6. eyebrows

   A. 1, 2, and 4
   B. 1, 3, and 4
   C. 3, 4, and 5
   D. 4, 5, and 6 ___

7. What type of current does Charlene's method use?

   A. galvanic
   B. direct
   C. low-frequency
   D. high-frequency ___

8. The angle at which she inserts a needle depends on the:

   A. angle at which the hair is growing.
   B. side of the body she is working on.
   C. shape of her needle.
   D. type of electrical current used. ___

---

9. Noel is temporarily removing his client's hair. Using depilatories, he has two choices from which to choose. They are:

   A. chemical and temporary.
   B. physical and permanent.
   C. permanent and electrolysis.
   D. physical and chemical. ___

10. Dao is using hot wax to remove hair from her client's face. She has applied the wax and the cloth strip. After it has cooled, she is to remove the strip:

   A. in the same direction as the hair growth.
   B. with a thermal needle.
   C. against the hair growth.
   D. slowly. ___

23. Cells, Anatomy, and Physiology

1. While performing a manicure, you accidentally cut your client with your cuticle nipper. The cuticle bleeds. The blood is part of which body system?

   A. excretory
   B. muscular
   C. skeletal
   D. circulatory ____

2. Huai has just completed a very difficult haircut on his client. As he looks at it, he feels excited and proud of his work. The tissue that carried these positive messages to his brain is ______________ tissue.

   A. muscular
   B. nerve
   C. connective
   D. epithelial ____

SITUATION FOR ITEMS 3-6:

Mark is performing an arm and hand massage on his manicuring client Rose.

3. Another name for Rose's fingers is:

   A. radii.
   B. carpi.
   C. metacarpus.
   D. digits. ____

4. The bones that he feels in Rose's fingers and thumbs are known as:

   A. phalanges.
   B. thorax.
   C. digits.
   D. zygomatic. ____

5. The muscle that causes Rose's fingers to separate, or spread apart, is the ____________ muscle.

   A. adductor
   B. opponent
   C. abductor
   D. supinator ___

6. The nerve that is on the little finger side of Rose's arm and in her palm is the ____________ nerve.

   A. ulnar
   B. radial
   C. median
   D. digital ___

---

7. Sabrina is an esthetician. This means that she must have a thorough understanding of the skin and its structures—its glands, nerves, layers, and appendages. This system that Sabrina is familiar with is the ____________ system.

   A. vascular
   B. integumentary
   C. excretory
   D. endocrine ___

8. When doing a wedge-style haircut on his client, Jeremey leaves a weight line at a bone above the nape area. The name of this bone is:

   A. parietal.
   B. ethmoid.
   C. sphenoid.
   D. occipital. ___

SITUATION FOR ITEMS 9–17:

Shelly is massaging Duane's face (her client) during a facial service. As she massages, she can feel different structures beneath Duane's skin surface. Duane is breathing slowly through his nose. He is almost asleep.

9. The two bones that form the bridge of his nose are the ____________ bones.

   A. lacrimal
   B. zygomatic
   C. nasal
   D. malar ___

10. The muscles that open and close Duane's mouth are:
    1. buccinator
    2. masseter
    3. triangularis
    4. temporalis
    5. auricularis superior

    A. 1 and 3
    B. 2 and 4
    C. 3 and 5
    D. 4 and 5

    ____

11. Duane's forehead, scalp, eyebrow, and upper eyelid are affected by which nerve?

    A. infra-trochlear
    B. infra-orbital
    C. supra-orbital
    D. supra-trochlear

    ____

12. Duane's inferior labial artery supplies blood to his:

    A. lower lip.
    B. chin.
    C. temples.
    D. forehead.

    ____

13. The sweat and oil glands on Duane's face are part of the ________________ system.

    A. nervous
    B. excretory
    C. digestive
    D. endocrine

    ____

14. Shelly is working on Duane's facial muscles. The study of muscles is known as:

    A. neurology.
    B. histology.
    C. myology.
    D. trichology.

    ____

15. Duane's inhalation and exhalation through his nose refer to his ________________ system.

    A. respiratory
    B. vascular
    C. nervous
    D. reproductive

    ____

16. Air is inhaled into two spongy tissues called the:
    A. kidneys.
    B. lungs.
    C. stomach.
    D. thorax. ___

17. Every time that Shelly and Duane exhale, they are expelling:
    A. carbon monoxide.
    B. oxygen.
    C. hydrogen.
    D. carbon dioxide. ___

---

18. As you walk your client to the shampoo bowl, you are using your voluntary muscles. Another name for this type of muscle tissue is:
    A. striated.
    B. nonstriated.
    C. involuntary.
    D. cardiac. ___

19. What carries water, food, oxygen, and secretions to every cell of Ryan's body?
    A. lymph
    B. perspiration
    C. blood
    D. platelets ___

20. Your facial client is a professional football player. The muscles on his neck and shoulders are extremely tight and need to be loosened. All of the following may be used to relax his muscles **EXCEPT**:
    A. massage.
    B. PABA.
    C. high-frequency current.
    D. infrared rays and moist heat. ___

SITUATION FOR ITEMS 21–24:

Roger is placing his roller set client under the dryer. The client has high blood pressure and is on medication. Heat that is too intense will increase the activity of her heart and may also increase her blood pressure.

21. The condition of this client pertains to her __________ system.

    A. respiratory
    B. circulatory
    C. temperature regulation
    D. nervous ___

22. The heart is a/an:

    A. nerve.
    B. bone.
    C. muscle.
    D. appendage. ___

23. At the normal resting rate, how many times per minute should the heart beat?

    A. 50–58
    B. 52–68
    C. 72–80
    D. 84–92 ___

24. What carries blood to the client's heart?

    A. veins
    B. capillaries
    C. arteries
    D. platelets ___

---

25. It has been a very busy day in the salon for you. It is 2:30 P.M. and you finally have time for a quick lunch break. You know that your food intake is part of the digestive system. What changes your food into a form so that your body can use it? Digestive:

    A. catalysts.
    B. lymph nodes.
    C. activators.
    D. enzymes. ___

24. Electricity and Light Therapy

1. You have a battery-operated radio at your salon station. The type of electricity you have is:

   A. direct current.
   B. a voltage.
   C. alternating current.
   D. a complete circuit. ___

SITUATION FOR ITEMS 2–3:

Your blow dryer puts out 10 amps of current and your thermal pressing oven puts out 40 amps.

2. Which of the following is true concerning the electrical cord of these implements? The:

   A. blow dryer needs a thicker cord.
   B. oven needs a thicker cord.
   C. blow dryer needs a circuit breaker.
   D. oven needs a thinner cord. ___

3. If the current is too strong, the:

   A. implement might not operate.
   B. wires will increase the circuit.
   C. wires can burn out.
   D. implement will not operate at full strength. ___

---

4. The electricity used in the Curl Up and Dye Salon is measured in:

   A. amperes.
   B. watts.
   C. volts.
   D. kilowatt hours. ___

5. While performing a facial, Terry uses a glass tube that conducts electricity from the facial machine to his client's skin. This glass tube is known as a/an:

   A. volt.
   B. watt.
   C. electrode.
   D. kilowatt hour. ___

6. Luke is using an anode on his client's skin in order to harden the tissues. What type of polarity does an anode have?

   A. negative
   B. positive
   C. alkaline
   D. increasing ___

7. Myrtis is using a process on her client that will soften and liquify oil in the pores and follicles. The process she is using is called:

   A. disincrustation.
   B. anaphoresis.
   C. phoresis.
   D. cataphoresis. ___

SITUATION FOR ITEMS 8–11:

Myong is performing a high-frequency current on his client's face and scalp.

8. Another name for this type of current is:

   A. galvanic.
   B. faradic.
   C. sinusoidal.
   D. tesla. ___

9. The main action of the current Myong is using is:

   A. a slow oscillation rate.
   B. the use of two or more electrodes.
   C. heat-producing.
   D. muscle contractions. ___

10. The shape of the electrode Myong uses on his client's scalp is:

    A. flat.
    B. rake.
    C. round.
    D. stick. ___

11. Myong should not use this type of current on all of his clients. On which of the following can Myong use a higher frequency current? A person who has, or is:

A. congestion.
B. pregnant.
C. many fillings in their teeth.
D. a pacemaker. ___

SITUATION FOR ITEMS 12–15:

Shane is under a lamp that has a reddish glow.

12. The type of rays Shane is exposing his skin to are __________ rays.

A. visible
B. ultra violet
C. blue
D. infrared ___

13. Of all the rays, the ones on Shane's skin produce the most:

A. heat.
B. light.
C. amount of color.
D. germicidal effects. ___

14. In order to obtain the best results and give Shane the maximum protection, the lamp should be kept __________ inches from Shane's skin.

A. 5
B. 10
C. 15
D. 30 ___

15. Shane's skin will experience all of the following **EXCEPT** a/an:

A. increase in blood circulation.
B. decrease in blood circulation.
C. relaxation.
D. soothing to his nerves. ___

SITUATION FOR ITEMS 16–18:

Cecilia is under an ultra violet lamp to treat her acne and dandruff.

16. What type of ultra violet ray has the most germicidal effect on the skin?

    A. UVA
    B. UVB
    C. UVC
    D. UVD
    ___

17. Another name for ultra violet rays is/are ___________ rays.

    A. actinic
    B. heat
    C. faradic
    D. infrared
    ___

18. All of the following are benefits of Cecilia's treatment **EXCEPT** an increase in:

    A. elimination if waste products.
    B. the risk of skin cancer.
    C. iron and vitamin D.
    D. circulation.
    ___

19. When performing light therapy on clients, you are to protect their:

    A. ears.
    B. faces.
    C. eyes.
    D. hands.
    ___

20. Your salon has two tanning beds in it. What type of light ray do the beds have?

    A. infrared
    B. UVC
    C. UVB
    D. UVA
    ___

25. Chemistry

SITUATION FOR ITEMS 1–5:

You are going to mix a bottle of permanent hair color with hydrogen peroxide. Before mixing them, you perform a pH test using litmus paper. Blue litmus paper turned red with the hydrogen peroxide, while red litmus paper turned blue with the hair color.

1. How many parts of oxygen are in hydrogen peroxide?
   A. one
   B. two
   C. three
   D. four ___

2. What type of compound is hydrogen peroxide?
   A. oxide
   B. alkali
   C. base
   D. salt ___

3. What type of change occurs when you mix permanent hair color with hydrogen peroxide?
   A. physical
   B. chemical
   C. acidic
   D. element ___

4. The litmus paper test tells you that the permanent hair color is a/an:

   1. base
   2. acid
   3. alkaline substance
   4. neutral substance

   A. 1 and 4
   B. 1 and 3
   C. 2 and 3
   D. 3 and 4 ___

5. The blue litmus paper which turned red means that hydrogen peroxide is a/an:

   A. acid.
   B. salt.
   C. alkaline substance.
   D. suspension. ___

SITUATION FOR ITEMS 6–9:

Bonnie is your client. She has an appointment for a shampoo, permanent wave, roller set, haircut, and temporary rinse.

6. What is the pH of Bonnie's natural hair?

   A. 1.0–2.5
   B. 3.5–4.5
   C. 4.5–5.5
   D. 7.0–8.5 ___

7. The alkaline cold wave you will use on her has a pH of:

   A. 3.5–5.5.
   B. 6.0–7.0.
   C. 9.0–9.5.
   D. 13.5–14.0. ___

8. The pure water you use to rinse her hair has a pH of:

   A. 1.5–3.5.
   B. 4.5–5.5.
   C. 7.0.
   D. 10.5–12.0. ___

9. The temporary color rinse you apply to her hair has a pH that is:

   A. 14.0.
   B. neutral.
   C. alkaline.
   D. acidic. ____

---

10. Tracy's shampoo is for dry, brittle hair. This means that the detergent in it is most likely to be:

    A. quaternary ammonium compound/s.
    B. sodium lauryl sulfate.
    C. cationics.
    D. sodium laureth sulfate. ____

11. Kelsey is 3 months old. To prevent her eyes from stinging, the shampoo used on her should have which type of detergent in it?

    A. nonionic
    B. cationic
    C. anionic
    D. ampholyte ____

SITUATION FOR ITEMS 12–15:

You are giving a permanent wave to Robert's hair. The perm is a thio solution. The hair is wrapped, processed, rinsed, and neutralized.

12. Which bonds must be broken and rearranged in order for Robert's perm to be successful?

    A. disulfide
    B. hydrogen
    C. bromate
    D. salt ____

13. In which layer of Robert's hair are these bonds found?

    A. cuticle
    B. cortex
    C. medulla
    D. epidermis ____

14. The neutralizer used on Robert's hair may contain the following chemical:

    A. ammonium thioglycolate.
    B. sodium hydroxide.
    C. hydrogen peroxide.
    D. lauryl sulfate. ____

15. The pH of the neutralizer that you use on Robert will be:

   A. 2.0–6.0.
   B. 7.0.
   C. 8.5–9.5.
   D. 10.0–14.0. ___

---

16. Jared is setting his client's wet hair on rollers. The set will last longer if he sets the hair while it is wet rather than dry. This is because:

   A. wet hair has greater porosity.
   B. dry hair has increased elasticity.
   C. the medulla opens up when hair is wet.
   D. hydrogen bonds break when hair is wet. ___

SITUATION FOR ITEMS 17–21:

Oscar and Helen want their hair colored. Oscar prefers a product that is not a strong chemical. Helen would like a semi-permanent color. You choose to use henna on Oscar and a polymer semi-permanent color for Helen.

17. The type of color product you use on Oscar is a/an ________________ tint.

   A. oxidation
   B. vegetable
   C. metallic
   D. compound ___

18. Oscar's henna will:

   A. last for 1 week.
   B. be permanent.
   C. last until his next shampoo.
   D. fade as he shampoos it. ___

19. In order for Helen's polymer color to process on her hair, it will be necessary to apply:

   A. a catalyst.
   B. ultra violet rays.
   C. heat.
   D. hydrogen peroxide. ___

20. The polymers in Helen's color may be made out of any of the following **EXCEPT**:

    A. glass.
    B. vinyl.
    C. plastic.
    D. human tissue. ___

21. One thing that the colors you use on Oscar and Helen have in common is that they both:

    A. oxidize.
    B. penetrate into the medulla.
    C. coat the hair.
    D. are aniline derivatives. ___

---

22. You have been using an aniline derivative tint on Courtney's hair for many years. Her ends have gotten too dark with a build-up of color on them. What should you use to remove this color build-up?

    A. hair lightener
    B. dye solvent
    C. compound dye
    D. lawsome ___

23. The foundation you want to apply during a makeup service has separated in its bottle. It needs to be shaken before you can use it. A product that has separated is called:

    A. a suspension.
    B. an emulsion.
    C. an ointment.
    D. immiscible. ___

SITUATION FOR ITEMS 24–26:

The directions for your disinfectant solution tell you to use a tablespoon of disinfectant for each cup of water.

24. In this mixture, water is the:

    A. emulsifier.
    B. binder.
    C. fixative.
    D. solvent. ___

25. The disinfectant is considered to be a:

A. solvent.
B. binder.
C. solute.
D. gas. ___

26. When using these proportions, you have made a/an ______________ solution.

A. dilute
B. even
C. concentrated
D. saturated ___

---

27. The thick setting lotion that you use on Ms. Hammer's hair is an example of a/an:

A. fatty acid.
B. mucilage.
C. ointment.
D. depilatory. ___

SITUATION FOR ITEMS 28–30:

Charles's hair is chemically relaxed with a sodium hydroxide product. Jackie's hair has been straightened with a thio product.

28. What is the pH of the product used on Charles?

A. 1.5–3.5
B. 7.0
C. 8.5–9.5
D. 13.0–14.0 ___

29. Which of the following is true concerning Charles and Jackie?

A. Charles may have his hair permanently curled
B. Jackie may have her hair permanently curled
C. Charles may get a thio relaxer today
D. Jackie may get a sodium hydroxide relaxer today ___

30. When hair is chemically relaxed, which bonds are broken? The ______________ bonds.

A. peptide
B. poly
C. disulfide
D. salt ___

---

31. Your permanent hair color client has 4 inches of natural, virgin hair, and then 5 inches of lightened, brittle hair toward the ends. This person wants their hair tinted back to its natural color. Before applying the tint, you apply a:

A. filler.
B. toner.
C. drabber.
D. fixative. ___

32. When performing a lightener retouch, you may use any of the following lighteners **EXCEPT** a/an ___________ lightener.

A. oil
B. cream
C. liquid
D. powder ___

33. The alcohol that you use to sanitize metal implements evaporates easily and quickly. A substance that evaporates quickly and easily is called:

A. miscible.
B. volatile.
C. PABA.
D. immiscible. ___

26. The Salon Business

1. Tammy, Stuart, Mai, and Quang are all part owners of Shear Image Salon. What type of ownership does this salon, with a state charter, have?

   A. individual
   B. partnership
   C. corporation
   D. joint

   ___

SITUATION FOR ITEMS 2–6:

The New Look Salon has been owned by Ret for 10 years. Chantha is buying it from Ret. They are in the process of negotiating the sale and would like it completed within 6 weeks. Chantha will be the sole owner.

2. Their agreement should include all of the following **EXCEPT**:

   A. a written purchase agreement.
   B. an inventory statement.
   C. a guarantee of profits to be made.
   D. the owner's identity.

   ___

3. In this situation, Chantha should hire a:

   A. manager.
   B. lawyer.
   C. podiatrist.
   D. licensed cosmetologist.

   ___

4. Chantha's type of ownership will be:

   A. individual.
   B. joint.
   C. partnership.
   D. corporation.

   ___

5. The federal law that both Ret and Chantha must follow include:

   A. county real estate tax.
   B. OSHA requirements.
   C. state sales tax.
   D. local zoning ordinances. ___

6. The salon insurance Chantha buys includes fire, burglary, theft, business interruption, and:

   A. homeowner's.
   B. automobile.
   C. whole life.
   D. malpractice. ___

---

7. Tiffany, the salon's owner, is figuring out her salon's expenses. In doing this, she determines that for every $100.00 that comes into her salon, her greatest expense is paying her employee's salaries. Approximately how much out of the hundred dollars does she pay them?

   A. $25.00
   B. $40.00
   C. $50.00
   D. $80.00 ___

SITUATION FOR ITEMS 8–10:

Poppy owns a salon, but is not a licensed cosmetologist. She rents space in a downtown building from Doris, the building owner. Poppy employs Franco to manage the salon. Franco has just hired Hiroko and Ramon to work in the salon.

8. The lease for the salon is a written agreement between Poppy and:

   A. Doris.
   B. Franco.
   C. Hiroko.
   D. Ramon. ___

9. When Franco was interviewing prospective employees for the salon, he considered all of the following **EXCEPT** their:

   A. personality.
   B. cosmetology skills.
   C. existing clients.
   D. age. ___

10. How many people Franco hired depended on the:

A. amount of money the salon had.
B. lack of salon clients.
C. amount of products in the salon.
D. size of the salon. ___

---

11. Your tint retouch client is paying for the service before leaving the salon. You mixed the hair color from the supplies in the salon's dispensary. What type of supply is the hair color used considered to be?

A. consumption
B. equipment
C. retail
D. wholesale ___

12. You would like to own your own salon. When planning this future goal, you must consider all of the following **EXCEPT** the:

A. state's public nuisance laws.
B. location.
C. amount of investment money you have.
D. available parking. ___

13. Corinne and Gene own the Hair Flair Salon together. They each own 50% of this salon. This type of ownership is called:

A. individual.
B. partnership.
C. corporate.
D. chain salon. ___

14. Sara lives in a friendly residential neighborhood in a large city. She would like to buy the house next door and turn it into a salon. Before she does this, however, she should check with her city's:

A. police department.
B. zoning ordinances.
C. renovation codes.
D. income tax laws. ___

SITUATION FOR ITEMS 15–18:

Dawn is the full-time receptionist at The Family Hair Care Salon. It is a large salon with 25 licensed cosmetologists on its payroll. Dawn is responsible for answering the telephone, handling the cash register, greeting clients, informing stylists when their clients have arrived, and much more.

15. If Dawn receives a complaint by telephone, she should do all of the following **EXCEPT**:

    A. listen to the entire problem.
    B. use a sympathetic voice.
    C. ask the client how the salon can remedy the situation.
    D. inform the client that nothing can be done. ___

16. When booking appointments for the many cosmetologists, Dawn should book them:

    A. every hour on the hour.
    B. according to the time they've worked at the salon.
    C. by using efficient use of their time.
    D. with as many clients as she can. ___

17. Which of the following practices should Dawn use on the telephone?
    1. answer it abruptly
    2. answer it promptly
    3. speak in a pleasant voice
    4. talk with someone standing by her
    5. be polite and interested
    6. let it ring six times before answering it

    A. 1, 3, and 4
    B. 2, 4, and 6
    C. 2, 3, and 5
    D. 4, 5, and 6 ___

18. A client wants to get a relaxer done this Friday at 10:30 A.M. by Marshall. Marshall is already booked with other request clients for that time. Trying to please this client, the receptionist, Dawn, should:

    A. suggest that the client go to a different salon.
    B. tell the client to leave the salon.
    C. tell the client that Marshall no longer does relaxers.
    D. suggest another time when Marshall is available. ___

SITUATION FOR ITEMS 19–20:

The owner of your salon has brought five different product lines into the salon. The owner would like each employee to sell at least $200.00 of these various products (shampoos, conditioners, hair spray, styling gels, skin creams, etc.) each week. The owner will pay you a percentage of each product that you sell.

19. What type of salon products are these considered to be?
    A. wholesale
    B. retail
    C. consumption
    D. equipment
    ___

20. In order for you to sell these products, you should:
    1. be familiar with all of them
    2. show the client how to use the product
    3. assume the client knows nothing about products
    4. have confidence in the product
    5. inform your clients that you must sell $200.00 worth of products

    A. 1, 2, and 4
    B. 1, 3, and 5
    C. 2, 3, and 4
    D. 3, 4, and 5
    ___

A removable answer key and scoring guide follow.

Made in the USA
Monee, IL
25 May 2021

69449578R00105